Community Indicators

Rhonda Phillips, AICP

TABLE OF CONTENTS

Community Indicators

Community indicators are measurements that provide information about past and current trends and assist planners and community leaders in making decisions that affect future outcomes. They can incorporate citizen involvement and participation. In essence, indicators are measurements that reflect the interplay between social, environmental, and economic factors affecting a region's or community's well-being. As such, they can be extremely valuable to planners. Community indicators projects typically are conducted by nonprofit organizations within a community, although in some cases they are initiated by the public sector. Community indicators are not new; rather, they have been in existence since 1910, when the Russell Sage Foundation initiated the development of local surveys for measuring industrial, educational, recreational, and other factors (Cobb and Rixford 1998, 6). The processes used by the Sage Foundation are similar to those that reemerged during the 1990s. But what is new is the use of indicators to consider the full spectrum of a community's well-being, not just isolated factors. So too, indicators are now used by many constituencies within a community. After a decade of renewed attention to community indicators, they now represent a valuable mechanism to improve monitoring and evaluation in planning.

1

This report reviews the evolution of community indicators since the early twentieth century and examines their implications for planning practice. It first defines what a community indicator is and how it should be used. It then explores the relationship between indicators and citizen participation, quality-of-life considerations, and sustainable development. A summary of the types and scale of indicators follows. The report also describes the process of identifying, selecting, and developing community indicators. That section draws on several applications from rural and urban environments to illustrate the process, with examples of how proponents designed the indicators and, more importantly, how planners have used them in their practice. Various considerations are then discussed, including the issues of data sharing and presentation. The report concludes with a list of annotated resources and links to encourage further exploration of community indicators as land-use planning tools.

DEFINITIONS

Community indicators are bits of information that, when combined, generate a picture of what is happening in a local system. They provide insight into the overall direction of a community: whether it is improving, declining, or staying the same, or is some mix of all three (Andrews 1996; Redefining Progress 1997). Indicators are gauges for a community, like the Dow Jones Industrial Average: just as the Dow indicates the direction of the whole stock market by tracking a small selection of stocks, indicators represent a whole community through a few factors, often selected by way of a community visioning process.

A combination of indicators can therefore provide a measuring system to provide information about past trends, current realities, and future direction in order to aid decision making (Hart 2003; Oleari 2000). In this sense, community indicators can also be thought of as grades on a report card that rates community well-being. Indicators may or may not be part of a benchmarking process (i.e., a process that establishes numeric goals to measure progress), although some indicator projects are used for this purpose. Indicators themselves do not provide a model of how a community works or how to determine planning choices; rather, they provide information that can be used by planners and others when faced with decisions about the community.

UNDERLYING PHILOSOPHY AND EVOLUTION

Policy makers have long used sets of information to aid in the decision-making process, just as community activists have used data to mobilize opinions so as to influence change. But as mentioned above, what today are called community indicators did not enter into use until around 1910 when the Russell Sage Foundation employed "over two thousand local surveys taken on education, recreation, public health, crime, and general social conditions" to assess social conditions (Cobb and Rixford 1998, 7). The first survey was conducted in Pittsburgh, Pennsylvania. (Interestingly, in the late 1990s, Pittsburgh has again embraced indicators, with its Sustainable Pittsburgh Goals and Indicators Project.) Many of the surveys used by the Sage Foundation were conducted by nonprofit organizations, such as chambers of commerce and citizen committees. These surveys yielded social trends indicators and were popular until the Great Depression and World War II, when economic measures such as the gross domestic product or gross national product indicators took greater precedence.

Interest in social trends emerged again during the social unrest of the 1960s when indicators—especially those that measured demographics, quality-of-life factors, and environmental quality—were thought to reveal

Community indicators are bits of information that, when combined, generate a picture of what is happening in a local system.

2

more about communities than traditional economic indicators. National and international governments and organizations took the lead this time, such as the U.S. Department of Health and Welfare. The use of indicators began to spread, and by the 1970s, researchers had produced a number of indicator-based studies.

Local and regional government soon after began to respond. One of the first examples came from the City of New York in its 1973 *Scorecard Project*. This project, financed by the Fund for the City of New York, reviewed a number of indicators that influence social well-being, such as education, health, and well-being. Although the original New York City project waned, as of 2003 a new project for providing data on key social and economic indicators emerged, the New York Social Indicators Project. This map-based system provides data about not only New York City but the state as a whole, and has been developed by the Lewis Mumford Center for Comparative Urban and Regional Research (2003).

At the state level, California's Office of Planning and Research published *Putting Social Indicators to Work: An Annotated Bibliography* in 1977. This work reviewed current research and indicators projects in an attempt to encourage local organizations and governments in California to identify and assess social indicators in their communities. Such use of indicators declined by the early 1980s, however, as policy analysts found indicators unable, through the descriptive statistical approach prevalent at the time, to adequately explain social phenomena (Cobb and Rixford 1998, 11).

In the late 1980s and early 1990s, advocates for indicator systems turned their attention to quality-of-life and overall community measures, incorporating concepts of well-being from economic, social, and environmental perspectives (Sawicki and Flynn 1996). During the 1990s, the emergence of the sustainability movement gave community indicators a new role in planning, policy, and citizen participation. The ideas behind and applications of community sustainability have been called a "virtual social movement," one that citizens and other stakeholders, private foundations, public agencies, and nonprofit national and international organizations have eagerly embraced (Innes and Booher 2000). Indeed, some recent publications that discuss community indicators attribute their development to the emergence of sustainable development approaches (Hart 2003; Anielski 2001).

Many communities interested in sustainability have incorporated indicators in their sustainability programs. These communities have found that the benefits of indicators projects include increased awareness of environmental needs and issues within the community. For example, the Martin County, Florida, community indicators project focuses on measuring the environmental "footprint" and sustainability of the county in direct relation to its natural, economic, and social resources. Building on the "design with nature" concepts pioneered by Ian McHarg, the ecological footprint model is a tool used to calculate the productive land required to sustain resource consumption and waste assimilation for a defined human population or economy (Hardi et al. 1997; Wackernagel and Rees 1996). The measurement the model yields shows how much land a person, city, or nation needs to sustain life. For example, the ecological footprint for the city of Vancouver is 14 times the actual area of the city (Greater Vancouver Regional District 2001).

More communities throughout Canada and the United States are beginning to apply the ecological footprint model as part of sustainable development efforts. Currently, however, more metropolitan than rural areas are applying the concepts of community indicators systems in the context of sustainable development. Little information exists about rural efforts to design and implement community indicators systems, although the needs

Many communities interested in sustainability have incorporated indicators in their sustainability programs.

in rural areas are just as pervasive as in metropolitan areas (Center for Building Better Communities 2001). But more attention is now being directed toward rural efforts, as evidenced by such recent projects as the Central Texas Sustainability Indicators Project, the Pueblo Community Indicators Project by the Healthy Pueblo Communities 2010 organization, and the Northern New England Sustainable Community Project by the Maine Community Foundation (International Institute for Sustainable Development 2003).

COMMUNITY PROGRAMS AND SPONSORS USING INDICATORS TO HELP MEASURE SUSTAINABILITY

- Sustainable Metro Jackson (Mississippi 2020 Network Inc.)

- Indicators for a Sustainable San Mateo County (Sustainable San Mateo County, California)

- Department Sustainable Community Initiative (City of Austin, Texas, Planning and Environmental Conservation Services)

- What Matters in Greater Phoenix: Indicators of Our Quality of Life (Arizona State University)

- Santa Monica Sustainable City Program (City of Santa Monica, California)

- Community Report Card (Sarasota County, Florida)

- Sustainable Seattle (Sustainable Seattle)

The four most common concerns that provide a framework for community indicator processes are quality of life, sustainability, performance evaluation, and healthy communities.

Research by planning professor Judith Innes (1998, 9), the director of the University of California's Institute of Urban and Regional Development, describes a far-reaching implication of designing and implementing a community indicators measuring system: indicators become more powerful once they are embedded in the practices and thinking of institutions and communities. Innes also argues that indicators can only exert influence if they represent "a socially constructed and shared understanding created in the community of policy actors"(p. 8). Community indicators measuring systems hold much potential not only as effective evaluation and monitoring systems, but also as mechanisms for effective social change.

THE CONTEXT FOR INDICATORS PROJECTS

The four most common concerns that provide a framework for community indicator processes are quality of life, sustainability, performance evaluation, and healthy communities. Of more than 200 community indicators projects described by Redefining Progress in its *The Community Indicators Handbook* (1997), 41 percent focus on quality of life, 37 percent on sustainability, 12 percent on performance evaluation, and 10 percent on a healthy communities model.

Quality of Life

Indicators for quality of life can be used to conceptualize what constitutes a "good life" or "good society." One model for thinking about valuation and indicators is utilitarianism, which holds that individuals maximize their quality of life based on the available resources and their individual desires (Diener and Suh 1997, 190). Most major indices of quality of life might be considered utilitarian, including the majority of commercial city and regional quality-of-life rankings, such as those found in *America's Top-Rated Cities* (Garoogian et al. 1998) and *Money Magazine's* ratings (e.g., *Money* 2003). These rankings assume the communities that offer the *most* resources—whether social, economic, or cultural—therefore offer the *highest* quality of life.

While utilitarianism dominates quality-of-life measures, there are limitations to its use as a guide for community indicators development. The biggest concern is that utilitarian indicators may not be linked to actions (Innes 1998). For example, a resident of a city ranked high on *Money's* most-livable-city list may experience a lower quality of life because the city's transit network does not allow the resident access to a high-paying job or the city's cultural district. The presence of resources, in other words, does not ensure active use of them: just because a city has a vibrant cultural district doesn't mean citizens will be able to make use of it.

Measuring quality of life can be tedious, conflicted, and uncertain. It is a political process because it involves competing ideologies that define what constitutes a "good life" in different ways. But those quality-of-life and indicators projects that try to remain above the political fray by excluding ideology or underlying philosophical premises are often not effective (Center for Building Better Communities 2001). Such projects also fail because, although the underlying premises of political participants may be in conflict (resulting in competing valuations in quality-of-life measures), these differences can make societies healthier (Cobb 2000).

Disagreements over the valuation of quality of life can be subsumed into four basic patterns, or value systems, that are in conflict with each other: hierarchy, isolation, sectarianism, and individualism (Douglas 1982). Those who conform to the pattern of hierarchy rely on traditional authority figures and therefore trust experts to provide the details of indicator systems. Isolationists "fatalistically assume that risk is unpredictable and that nothing can be done to avoid threats" and so do not engage in political or cultural debates (Cobb 2000, 23). Sectarians believe social order is under constant threat from elites who abuse power; they use indicators to show the social risks associated with unequal power and the need for more egalitarian institutions (Cobb 2000, 23). Individualists do not trust the "system" and believe risks can be overcome with self-regulating processes.

The conflicts between these value systems not only emphasize the differences between these approaches to valuation, but they also make clear how important it is for planners and other political actors to understand the process behind many valuation efforts. For example, efforts to develop social indicators that regard public discussion as an end in itself are often the product of a sectarian value system: discussion, according to this system, is valuable because it limits the concentration and abuse of power by making policy decisions subject to public debate. Yet the tolerance that necessarily accompanies this support for discussion—that all views are equal and must be accommodated so as to curb power—can be problematic. One researcher explains it this way:

> The effort to achieve neutrality and universal acceptance has been a recipe for preserving the status quo. If indicators are to promote the kind of reform that their proponents often seem to hope they will achieve, they will inevitably challenge accepted conventions and institutions. That may be less comfortable than designing indicators that avoid controversy, but no social progress can occur unless we accept the virtue of rational conflict. (Cobb 2000, 27)

Thus, the sectarian insistence on consensus may actually lead to the possibility that no agreement will be reached, that opportunities for dissent

Measuring quality of life . . . is a political process because it involves competing ideologies that define what constitutes a "good life" in different ways.

will be minimized, or that communities will fail to increase any resident's quality of life because their decision makers are too focused on accommodating every complaint.

Decision makers will be unable to achieve the balance necessary between consensus and productive rational conflict without understanding the value systems that underlie different community indicators. Any indicators project must incorporate research to identify successful indicators approaches that recognize these value systems and can productively mobilize their differences at the same time.

THE JACKSONVILLE, FLORIDA, COMMUNITY COUNCIL'S QUALITY-OF-LIFE INDICATOR PROJECT

A community's quality of life reflects values inherent to that community. If indicators are therefore understood as measurements of what a community cares about, indicators can shift, reinforce, or promote a particular set of values (Meadows 1998, 2). By integrating indicators into overall planning activities, a community makes clear that its residents' quality of life is of vital importance.

The nonprofit Jacksonville Community Council Inc. (JCCI) in Florida was the first to consistently use quality-of-life indicators in the United States. In 1974, roughly 100 delegates representing a cross-section of the population of northern Florida—business professionals, public office holders, laborers, and citizens—developed goals for the regional growth and development of Jacksonville. They chose 10 indicator categories and assigned task forces to study each. The categories were (and still are, with some name modifications): education, economy, public safety, natural environment, health, social environment, government and politics, culture and recreation, mobility, and transportation (Crooks 2000). With support from the Jacksonville Chamber of Commerce and the United Way, and now with the aid of local government, JCCI releases annual quality-of-life indexes.

Currently, about one-third of community indicators projects in the United States are based on the JCCI model. JCCI is considered to be a successful project: it is regarded as a well-respected community think tank (Besleme et al. 1999, 18), and its data, graphics, reports, and information are frequently used in the news media of the region.

Sustainable Development

First articulated by the World Commission on Environment and Development—also known as the Brundtland Commission—in 1987, the most widely accepted definition of sustainable development is: development that meets the needs of the present without compromising the ability of future generations to meet their own needs. Further, this definition can be expanded to include two other concepts: *needs*, in particular the basic needs of the world's poor, to which overriding priority should be given; and *limitations*, imposed by technology and social organization, on the environment's ability to meet present and future needs (Hardi et al. 1997, 2, emphasis added).

This definition emerged from concern that the world relies too heavily on economic measures of performance that do not reflect the complete spectrum of social and environmental well-being. It also grew from the idea that a "shift in the nature of human activities is required if life for future generations is to be as rich as that found currently" (Hardi and Zdan 1997, 7). Sustainable development contrasts with more traditional development driven by the needs inherent to measuring growth in terms of the most commonly recognized indicators used in the United States, the gross domestic product (GDP) and gross national product (GNP). GDP is the output of labor and property located within a country; GNP adds net income from abroad. Development policies aimed at upping these indicators are often not compatible with policies that promote sustainable development. As Mark Anielski (2001, 4) argues:

> Pursuit of goals for more GDP growth, more trade, competitive advantage and more monetary wealth is fundamentally at odds with the notion of sustaining or improving the conditions of living capital. . . . [I]n a world focused on the pursuit of monetary objectives and on measuring prosperity, is it any wonder that the words "sustainable" and "development" are problematic?

In 1996, an international group of practitioners and researchers, concerned with measuring and assessing progress towards sustainable development, convened in Bellagio, Italy. From this meeting, overseen by the International Institute for Sustainable Development (IISD) located in Winnipeg, Manitoba, came the Bellagio Principles for Assessment. These principles have exerted significant influence on subsequent sustainable development activities, policies, and study. The 10 Bellagio principles are:

1. Guiding Vision and Goals: develop a clear vision of sustainable development and goals to define that vision

2. Holistic Perspective: consider the well-being of social, ecological, and economic subsystems in monetary and nonmonetary terms

3. Essential Elements: consider equity and disparity issues, ecological conditions, economic development, and other nonmarket activities contributing to human and social well-being

4. Adequate Scope: adopt a time horizon long enough to capture both human and ecological time scales; build on historic and current conditions to anticipate future conditions

5. Practical Focus: generate explicit set of categories or organizing framework to link vision and goals to indicators and assessment criteria

6. Openness: make methods and data accessible to all; make explicit all judgments and assumptions in data and interpretations

7. Effective Communication: design to address needs of users; draw from indicators and other tools to engage decision makers

8. Broad Participation: provide for inclusive representation and participation

9. Ongoing Assessment: ensure capacity for repeated measurement; adjust goals and framework as new insights gained

10. Institutional Capacity: clearly assign responsibilities; support development of local assessment capacity (adapted from Hardi and Zdan 1997, 2–4)

Indicators are just one means—but potentially a particularly effective means—of measuring progress toward sustainable development in a manner consistent with these principles. Indicators offer an opportunity to go beyond a standard economic indicator, such as gross domestic product, to fully assess well-being.

Indicators offer an opportunity to go beyond a standard economic indicator, such as gross domestic product, to fully assess well-being.

TABLE 1
SEATTLE'S SUSTAINABILITY INDICATORS

Formed in 1990 by a group of volunteers from nonprofit, business, and environmental organizations in Seattle, Sustainable Seattle assesses the city's progress toward "long-term health and vitality" that is "cultural, economic, environmental, and social" (Besleme and Mullin 1997, 47). In 1995, the organization published its full report on its indicators, grouped under five main headings. These indicator categories include: environment, population and resources, economy, youth and education, and health and community. The report defines each indicator, interprets indicator data, describes the indicator's evolution over time, and analyzes the interconnections between the indicators, or links between them.

According to Redefining Progress (1997), more than half of the community indicators projects in the United States had modeled theirs after Sustainable Seattle. The popularity of this model continues today, with many communities replicating Seattle's success. The model has been widely adopted because citizens can easily understand how its indicators affect their daily lives. Furthermore, the idea of sustainable development continues to be alluring to communities. Sustainable Seattle's model is very much oriented towards measuring sustainability, with 40 specific measures across the five categories.

Sector	Issue/Indicator	Trend: Improving/Declining/ Neutral/Insufficient Data (ID)
Environment	Wild Salmon	Neutral
	Ecological Health	ID
	Soil Erosion	Neutral
	Air Quality	Improving
	Pedestrian- and Bicycle-Friendly Streets	ID
	Open Space Near Villages	ID
	Impervious Surfaces	ID
Population and Resources	Population	Neutral
	Water Consumption	Improving
	Solid Waste Generated and Recycled	Declining
	Pollution Prevention	Improving
	Local Farm Production	Declining
	Vehicle Miles Travelled and Fuel Consumption	Declining
	Renewable and Nonrenewable Energy Use	Declining

(continued)

Performance Evaluation

Oregon Benchmarks is a program begun by state government in 1989 that provides a set of goals to determine how efficiently Oregon is producing a workforce that can keep up with the demands of the global economy. The program has many unique features, including future targets for its indicators in the biophysical, economic, and social categories. The most critical indicators are divided into benchmarks classified as urgent (for immediate attention) and core (for long-term sustainability). These benchmarks are then incorporated into the state

TABLE 1
SEATTLE'S SUSTAINABILITY INDICATORS *(continued)*

Sector	Issue/Indicator	Trend: Improving/Declining/ Neutral/Insufficient Data (ID)
Economy	Energy Use per Dollar of Income	Improving
	Employment Concentration	Improving
	Unemployment	Improving
	Distribution of Personal Income	Declining
	Health Care Expenditures	Declining
	Work Required for Basic Needs	Declining
	Housing Affordability	Neutral
	Children Living in Poverty	Declining
	Emergency Room for Non-ER Purposes	Neutral
	Community Reinvestment	ID
Youth and Education	High School Graduation	ID
	Ethnic Diversity of Teachers	Neutral
	Arts Instruction	ID
	Volunteer Involvement in Schools	Improving
	Juvenile Crime	Improving
	Youth Involvement in Community Service	ID
	Equity in Justice	Improving
	Adult Literacy	ID
Health and Community	Low Birth Weight Infants	Neutral
	Asthma Hospitalization for Children	Neutral
	Voter Participation	Improving
	Library and Community Center Use	Neutral
	Public Participation in the Arts	Improving
	Gardening	Improving
	Neighborliness	ID
	Perceived Quality of Life	Neutral

budgeting process each year. Indicators are reviewed every two years by the Oregon Progress Board, which is overseen by the state's governor (see Oregon Progress Board 1992 and 2003). The most recent report, including errata, is available at www.econ.state.or.us/opb/2003report/ 2003BPR.htm

Since 1989, the program has matured from an indicators project to an integral part of state government. Because the project is used in budgeting and has direct linkage to state government, it is a good example of how indicators can be integrated into government actions.

Several other states have initiated projects using the Oregon model, including Minnesota, Montana, and Kansas (Hardi et al. 1997). Performance evaluation projects such as Oregon Benchmarks are unique in that they are initiated and developed by government. Citizens may participate through public meetings, but elected and appointed officials have final responsibility for developing the indicators.

Healthy Communities

Healthy communities projects attempt to cultivate a "sense of shared responsibility for community health and well-being" (Besleme and Mullin 1997, 43). These projects redefine traditional measures of healthy conditions and typically build upon the World Health Organization's (WHO) Healthy Cities program (Waddell 1995). The WHO indicators include measures such as air quality, access to medical care, and nutrition designed to gauge and compare citizens' health status across countries.

A variation of the WHO approach has been designed and implemented by Hampton, Virginia, with its Healthy Families Partnership. The city developed this program in 1992 to improve the parenting skills of citizens. Its goal is to reach out to parents from the time of pregnancy through preschool to develop their skills and to inform them how to access needed resources. Since its founding, the program has been a success: low-birthweight incidences have decreased, as have other problems. For example, there has been a 26.8 percent reduction in child abuse and neglect in Hampton compared to only a 3.4 percent reduction in the larger region, and a 96 percent immunization rate for toddlers in Hampton compared to the state of Virginia average of 73 percent (Nelson 2003). Children and parents participate in a variety of educational activities, all designed to encourage healthy childhood experiences.

One of the unanticipated outcomes of the Healthy Families Partnership is the economic development it has brought to Hampton.

One of the unanticipated outcomes of the Healthy Families Partnership is the economic development it has brought to Hampton. After the national media picked up the program's story, the city received significant interest from corporations that wanted to locate facilities there (Stein 2000). While there is not a formal study of these impacts, several companies have relayed to the Healthy Families Partnership staff that they selected Hampton because of the program and the perception of a community willing to invest in its citizens, potential future workers for these companies (Nelson 2003).

Hampton's success has prompted other communities throughout the United States to adopt similar frameworks, such as the Gainesville, Florida, Healthy Community Initiative (see also Association for Community Health Improvement 2003).

CITIZEN PARTICIPATION AND COMMUNITY INDICATORS

The strength of a community indicators measuring system lies in the involvement of citizens. The process of designing an indicators project can be invaluable to a community. By participating in the development of a project, residents can contribute to finding solutions to common problems. Bringing residents together to envision their community's future, establish specific goals, and select indicators for gauging progress can foster residents' sense of belonging to their community and encourage stronger interest in outcomes.

Citizen participation in the process of developing a community indicators project is critical at all levels, and particularly at the local level. Helping to identify and design indicators makes citizens more invested in their communities, and support is more likely to emerge when common goals are identified. While there does not appear to be any formal research on whether citizens stay involved after the initial process is completed, informal inquiry indicates that they do. For example, in Calgary, thousands of citizens have been involved in indicators projects since 1995. The establishment of common goals for which a community can measure progress often serves to diffuse conflicts within a community: if citizens can agree on goals, a basis of mutual understanding can be established and sustained.

Citizen participation can itself be treated as an indicator since low participation rates often reflect low quality of life. In its work with 21 pilot projects at the local level, the Toronto-based International Council for Local Environmental Initiatives has identified several factors that planners should consider when developing citizen participation indicators. These are described in Figure 1.

FIGURE 1. EXAMPLE OF CITIES 21 INDICATORS FOR CITIZEN PARTICIPATION

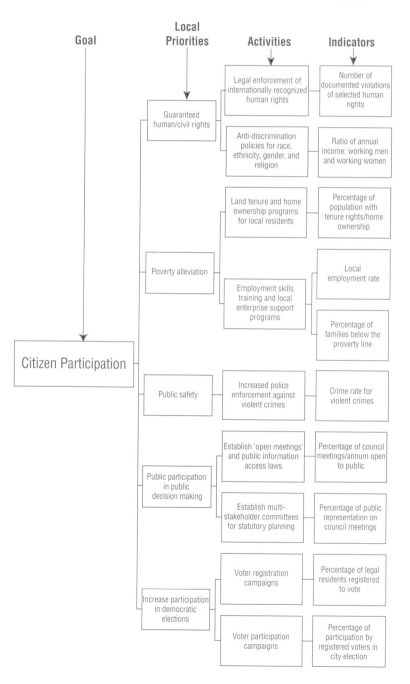

TYPES AND SCALE OF COMMUNITY INDICATORS
Types: System and Performance Indicators

There are two basic, very similar types of indicators: *system* (sometimes called *descriptive*) *indicators* and *performance indicators*. System indicators summarize individual measurements that describe multiple characteristics of a specific system—an ecosystem, for example, or a social system—and communicate the most relevant information to decision makers (Hardi et al. 1997). In other words, system indicators offer "vital information providing a picture about the current state and corresponding viability of that system" (Bossel 1999, 10). Often, system indicators are based on technical and scientific research and analysis. An example of a system indicator project would be assessing the environmental quality of a region.

There are, however, several limitations to system indicators:

> In the best case, information carried by system indicators would be determined by science. Unfortunately, the inherent uncertainties of natural systems usually make insistence on "beyond a doubt" proof impractical. Therefore, the standards and benchmarks to which indicators are related are determined only partially by science, and to a considerable degree by the policy process. Consequently, indicators themselves are also the products of a compromise between scientific accuracy and the needs of decision makers, and urgency of action. This limitation becomes quite clear in the social dimension where many of the variables, such as political stability, cultural aspirations, and equity, are hardly quantifiable and cannot even be defined in physical terms. Nevertheless, whatever level of accuracy is achieved in defining the indicators, it remains a realistic goal to measure them consistently and in a comparable manner across time, space, and organizations in order to determine trends. (Hardi et al. 1997, 9)

Planners often find systems indicators hard to accept since a variety of external factors influence indicators, and these factors are not controllable. Richard Gelb, director of Seattle's Office of Sustainability and Environment, explains: "Planners and others involved in implementation may be reticent to accept systems indicators because the bar is too high. It is asking them to accept responsibility for things they can only partially control" (Gelb 2002). Further, system indicators can be difficult to construct since many factors that contribute to a community's quality of life are not easily quantified and are even less easily verifiable (Bennett 2002).

Performance indicators, the second indicator type, are similar to system indicators in that both are descriptive: they describe a particular system. However, performance indicators are also prescriptive: they include a reference value or policy target that allows comparisons with local, national, or international goals, targets, and objectives. Thus performance indicators are particularly useful in the policy evaluation phase of the decision-making process (Hardi et al. 1997, 9). Often, performance indicators are used in the context of organizational or community goal setting. Indicators that establish certain economic development goals for a community—for example, increasing the number of jobs in the community by 5 percent in one year or attracting two new enterprises to downtown per year—are performance indicators.

One shortcoming of performance indicators is the difficulty of designing the indicator to realistically reflect the target or objectives. Making indicators very specific with targeted goals or benchmarks may not be a comfortable exercise. In other words, setting specific goals may be viewed as too limiting from the perspective of those who have to achieve the goal because to do so puts pressure on them if the goals are unrealistically high. In this sense, this limitation of performance indicators is similar to that of systems indicators.

There are two basic, very similar types of indicators: system (sometimes called descriptive) indicators and performance indicators.

In many situations, system and performance indicators are linked, leading to more effective evaluation and mitigating some of the difficulties described above. Often, community indicators projects incorporate both types in order to more fully reflect conditions in the area of study.

These two types of indicators are typically arranged under three basic categories:

1. Environmental

2. Economic

3. Social

These widely recognized categories are what some call the "triple bottom line" (Global Reporting Initiative 2003). Some organizations focus on one category for their indicators, while others combine all three.

The State of the Nation's Ecosystems project carried out by the Heinz Center for Science, Economics, and the Environment (2002) makes wide use of environmental indicators. The project is a comprehensive effort to establish a periodic and reliable compilation of information about the U.S.'s natural environment. Six major ecosystem types are used as the basis for reporting data and developing 15 to 20 indicators for each. The ecosystems are: urban and suburban areas, coasts and oceans, fresh waters, forests, grasslands and shrublands, and farmlands (Heinz Center for Science, Economics, and the Environment 2002, 9, 17). The 103 indicators form a core set of national-level data selected for their importance as determined by nearly 150 researchers working together over a five-year period. The next report in the series is expected in 2007.

Economic measures are often the focus of indicators studies, particularly those sponsored by economic development organizations at the state, regional, or local levels. The Maine Economic Growth Council, for example, annually updates its Measures of Growth project. Since 1993, the Council has tracked 60 performance measures. These include a variety of economic indicators, ranging from prosperity measures (jobs that pay a livable wage, household debt) to business innovation (internet connectivity, job growth among new businesses) and business climate (new products and services and other measures). The project also incorporates civic assets measures—which include, for example, business involvement in communities and schools—as well as indicators for skilled and educated workers (Maine Economic Growth Council 2003).

An example of an indicators project focused on the social category is the *2000/2001 Report on Social Indicators* by the New York City Department of City Planning (2002). The New York City report is a compendium of measures for gauging the social health of the city; while the focus is on social elements, though, it includes measures from other categories as well. Its approach is typical of most indicator projects, which often combine all three categories even if they tend to focus on one. The reason? All three categories of indicators are closely interrelated, and it is often impossible to analyze one aspect of a community or region without looking at the others.

Scale

Indicators can be almost infinitely scaled, but the national and multinational levels are probably the most commonly recognized. In the United States and Canada, regional approaches that focus on all or part of a state or states (or provinces) are also increasingly common. Metropolitan areas and counties often form the basis for local indicators projects, while neighborhood projects focus on specific, tightly defined areas of a city. It is important to note that governments are not always the initiators of indicator projects. California-based Redefining Progress, one of the first national-level organizations tracking community indicators projects, found in 1997 that almost half of the more than 200 indicator projects in the United States had been initiated by nongovernment organizations (Redefining Progress 1997). The goal of many of these organizations is to elicit participation from community residents and other organizations to identify and construct indicators to influence policy outcomes in the public sector.

National and multinational indicators. National and multinational indicator projects abound. Many large multinational agencies have major indicator projects, ranging from general international trend analysis to community-specific concerns. Such projects include the World Bank's Development Indicators program, the United Nations Center for Human Settlements' Global Urban Observatory, and the World Health Organization's Healthy Cities Project (ICLEI 2000, 1.1). A number of countries have also undertaken indicator projects, including Australia, the Netherlands, and Brazil.

Within Canada, long-term sustainability drives several approaches to indicator development. Following the Bellagio Principles, two public-sector organizations, Environment Canada and the National Round Table on the Environment and the Economy, are currently institutionalizing indica-

> *The goal . . . is to elicit participation from community residents and other organizations to identify and construct indicators to influence policy outcomes in the public sector.*

tors that aim to measure progress towards sustainable development. These projects are based primarily on performance indicators, which are used as a primary aid to decision making. As measures that join past and present activities to future goals, indicators therefore serve as these projects' basic tool.

Peter Hardi and others (1997, 7) summarize the benefits of this kind of measurement-based approach. First, they argue, this approach can help decision makers "understand what sustainable development means in operational terms." In this way, "measurement and indicators are explanatory tools, translating the concepts of sustainable development into practical terms." Second, this approach encourages decision makers to choose policies that embrace sustainable development. Through these policies, indicators can "create linkages between everyday activities and sustainable development." Thus they become *planning tools* because they "provide a sense of direction for decision makers when they choose between policy alternatives." Third, this approach helps decision makers "decide how successful efforts are to meet sustainable development goals and objectives," which means that indicators are performance assessment tools.

In the United States, the President's Council on Sustainable Development recommended the formation of the Interagency Working Group on Sustainable Development Indicators (SDI Group) in 1996. The SDI Group developed a framework that groups indicators into three categories:

1. endowments (capital or wealth, and liabilities);

2. driving processes and forces (savings/investment or disinvestment/ depreciation); and

3. current outputs and results (goods and services used, value derived by satisfying wants and needs) (U.S. Interagency 2001).

Projects that have a national or multinational focus draw on indicator data that is available for long periods of time, usually over several decades. The majority of indicators used in these projects are leading indicators or similar economic data. The 40 indicators included in Table 2 are those most widely used by the organizations described above; they represent what these organizations consider most important to measure and assess.

As these indicators suggest, national and multinational projects tend to be more general in their focus than community-based initiatives and thus may fail to translate indicators into actions.

Regional indicators. Environmental and sustainability concerns often drive regional efforts. One state-level project is Minnesota Milestones, begun in 1991, in which citizens helped to develop 79 indicators for measuring fulfillment of 20 short- and long-term goals. Some of these goals have been integrated into overall state planning activities. The state oversaw the development of the indicators process, which is still ongoing. The indicators are used to gauge progress toward goals in four categories: environment, people, community and democracy, and economy (Minnesota 2003).

Vermont has adopted an outcomes approach to measuring progress towards such goals as preservation of the state's natural and historic built resources. Several indicators have been developed for each goal, placing emphasis on achieving the desired outcomes (Murphy 1999). These desired outcomes can be very specific or more general, such as preserving a particular area of the state or developing supporting policies for preservation statewide. Indicators provide the data to measure the success of these policies.

Environmental and sustainability concerns often drive regional efforts.

TABLE 2

TABLE 2

EXAMPLE OF NATIONAL LEVEL INDICATORS DEVELOPED FOR THE UNITED STATES

Economic	Environmental	Social
Capital assets	Contaminants in biota	Access to telecommunications
Labor productivity	Timbergrowth-to-removals balance	Educational attainment by level
Total materials per unit of investment and per Personal Consumption Expenditures	Metropolitan air quality non-attainment	Life expectancy
		Educational achievement rates
Investment in research and development as a percentage of gross domestic product	Status of stratospheric ozone	Percentage of children living in poverty
	Greenhouse climate response index	Number of people in census tracts with 40 percent poverty
Economy management index	Greenhouse gas emissions	Citizen participation
Consumption and government expenditures per capita	Waste inventory	Access to health care
	Surface water quality	Homelessness
Home ownership	Land use	Population
Percentage of households with housing problems	Ratio of renewable water supply to withdrawals	Children living in families with at least one parent present
Vehicle ownership, fuel use, and travel per capita	Rate of use of fisheries	Crime rates
Percentage of renewable energy	Invasive alien species	Teacher training and applications of qualifications
	Soil erosion rates	
	Outdoor recreational activities	Wealth distribution
	Biodiversity	Contributing time and money to charities

Source: U.S. Interagency (2001).

The Pembina Institute considers its accounting standards innovative because they provide a holistic and integrated analysis of the physical, qualitative, and monetary dimensions of all living and produced capital.

In Canada, the Genuine Progress Indicators (GPI) System of Sustainable Well-Being Accounting, a new accounting standard developed by the Pembina Institute, was adopted by the Alberta provincial government in 2000. GPI accounting is a highly comprehensive assessment of the total health of a society, its economy, and the natural environment. Its developers intend it as an alternate to traditional accounting systems focused on calculating such measures as GDP and GNP. While GPI accounts are developed largely in accordance with traditional accounting standards, they add a synthesis of many existing measurement systems for human, natural, and social capital. The Pembina Institute considers its accounting standards innovative because they provide a holistic and integrated analysis of the physical, qualitative, and monetary dimensions of all living and produced capital (Anielski 2001, 3).

GPI accounting draws on raw time-series data from regional and local governments, statistical agencies, and other organizations to construct accounts of conditions of personal health, social cohesion, intellectual capital, economic prosperity, and the sustainability of natural capital and the health of the environment (Anielski 2001, 3). Fifty-one indicators comprise the system and are calculated by normalizing raw data on a scale from 1 to 100 (with 1 as the poorest condition over time and 100 the best). Longitudinal data are used against a selected benchmark. For example, in the Economic Well-Being Category, 12 indicators are selected and followed from 1961 to the most recent year's data. These indicators include traditional economic measures such as real GDP per capita as well as measures of transportation expenditures and public infrastructure. An overall score for the category indicates where Alberta is at any given time: for example, in 1999 the province's economic well-being score was 63—higher than previous years—while its social well-being was 67. Remember the ecological footprint model discussed above? Alberta includes this as one of the measures of environmental well-being. The ecological footprint of each citizen in Alberta has increased at a rate of 1.4 percent per annum, with the 1999 footprint six times larger than the average global carrying capacity rating (Anielski 2001, 35). That rate of increase contributed to the province's score of 44 in its GPI Condition Index.

What does all this mean for planners? Because the aggregate scores for economic and social well-being are higher than for environmental well-being, environmental policies and activities merit more attention lest further declines occur in the measures. The idea of ecological footprint, for example, might be translated into design standards that use fewer natural resources.

Local indicators. As the former director of the Community Indicators Network at Redefining Progress, Kate Besleme, explains, local indicator projects usually come about when "multiple needs, purposes, and concerns of individual stakeholders converge into an overarching question about how the community as a whole is doing and whether it is headed in a desirable direction. . . . [I]ndicators projects operate under the assumption that community well-being can be defined and measured, and then managed and preserved" (Besleme et al. 1999, 1).

There are currently hundreds of cities and towns designing and implementing indicators projects. They range from the large-scale, still ongoing Quality of Life project in Jacksonville, Florida, begun in 1985 to projects for small towns, such as Banff in Alberta. Some larger American cities have comprehensive programs, such as the Sustainable Boston program, as do many counties, such as Pierce County in Washington, which through its Department of Community Services publishes the annual report *Pierce County Quality of Life Benchmarks*. Some local governments combine to develop indicators for a region, as do the eight counties that constitute the Kansas City metropolitan area; likewise, many small cities on Cape Cod in Massachusetts have cooperated to produce the annual report *The Pulse of Cape Cod: Measuring Progress for Sustainability*. Planners are involved in these projects in various ways, from providing data to participating in the indicator selection process. The public sector projects, such as Pierce County's, include planners and try to relate their work to planning activities, while the nonprofit projects encourage the public sector to use the indicators whenever possible in planning activities.

Neighborhood indicators. Planners have long understood the value of recurrently updated indicators that reflect changing neighborhood conditions in their cities (Kingsley 1998, 1). However, not until the 1990s did advancing technology in data accessibility and applicability (such as geographic information systems) allow realistic and effective analysis at the neighborhood level. Indicators developed for use at the neighborhood level include measures of vacant housing and crime as well as of organizing resources and capacity building for the community. (These latter two mea-

Planners have long understood the value of recurrently updated indicators that reflect changing neighborhood conditions in their cities.

sures include such items as civic participation rates, community leadership development programs, and the types of organizations that exist.) Because these indicators can help a community recognize its physical and social resources, they have often been used to support citywide initiatives. The National Neighborhood Indicators Project (NNIP), a collaborative effort with the Urban Institute, is working to help neighborhoods establish indicators projects through its local partnership program. A wealth of information has been collected by the NNIP from 28 neighborhoods throughout the United States that are using indicators for a variety of projects ranging from reforming the handling of tax-delinquent properties in neighborhoods of Providence, Rhode Island, to facilitating neighborhood-based service delivery in Cleveland.

CRITERIA FOR SELECTING SUCCESSFUL INDICATORS

While specific indicators will vary depending on a community's needs and desires, there are several common criteria for choosing indicators. Justin Hollander (2002, 3) has identified nine of the most common criteria for selecting indicators:

1. Validity: well grounded in sound data and accurately depicts a real situation

2. Relevance: appropriate for and pertinent to the community's important issues

3. Consistency and reliability: data can be researched reliably over a period of time

4. Measurability: data can be obtained for the community

5. Clarity: unambiguous; understandable by a diverse group of people

6. Comprehensiveness: represents many parts of an issue and reduces the need for an excessive number of indicators

7. Cost-effectiveness: data collection is not overly expensive

8. Comparability: sufficiently general that communities can be compared to one another

9. Attractiveness to the media: the press is likely to embrace it

These qualities tend to be reflected in many current community indicators projects across the United States and Canada, with emphasis varying depending on the desires and preferences of individual communities. Yet this list is not exhaustive: an indicator should also have a conceptual basis that makes clear exactly what is being measured. As Clifford Cobb and Craig Rixford (1998, 16) explain,

> This [conceptual clarity] may seem like obvious advice, but it is not easy to follow in practice. There is an understandable tendency for groups intent on developing indicators to start compiling data right away without a clear understanding of what needs to be measured. Taking the time to develop conceptual clarity seems to many people a kind of useless intellectual exercise; however, . . . a lack of clarity can lead to endless problems. Although measurement can help clarify a concept, the concept itself will not simply emerge from the data.

A successful indicator should also:

• be appropriate to its political, institutional, jurisdictional, or other contexts;

An indicator should also have a conceptual basis that makes clear exactly what is being measured.

- be meaningful and useful to stakeholders;

- use affordable, relevant, and accessible data sources;

- clearly state and accurately reflect its intent;

- result from close collaboration with stakeholders during selection, application, and review processes; and

- connect and be consistent with well-articulated vision statements and goals (Seasons 2001, 9).

Most importantly, however, a successful indicator is one that causes a government *to take action*. Many past indicator projects failed, particularly in the 1960s and 1970s, because local jurisdictions took no action after identifying indicators (Innes 1998; Sawicki and Flynn 1996). These projects, which were primarily centered on system indicators, were not sufficient to survive long-term because the data were not used as a basis for subsequent actions. Some critics today fear that these failures have been replicated in the indicator projects of the 1990s and 2000s (Cobb 2002). Supporters, however, see the promise of much more explicit and applied, and thus successful, government action. While the verdict is still out on the long-term survivability of today's indicators projects, the widespread and continued use of indicators by many communities will likely increase their longevity and usefulness.

IMPLICATIONS FOR PLANNING

According to Kate Besleme and Megan Mullin (1997, 47), indicators are "simply measurements that reflect the status of larger systems." Yet, if they are simply measurements, why should planners consider their use? After all, many measurements currently exist, as evidenced by the integration of myriad data into planning reports.

The answer to the question lies in a well-worn adage: the whole is greater than the sum of its parts. In other words, indicators represent a group of data that by their very formulation establish goals and visions of the community and that community members can use to facilitate change. "Community indicators drive change," stated Thomas Kingsley (2002) of the Urban Institute, who directs the National Neighborhood Indicators Project, an indicators research and education initiative with 19 community partners. By providing information about past and current trends, community indicators are essentially a balance sheet for a community—a reckoning between the community's collective values and its actions toward achieving those values. Indicators also serve as one means to democratize data, providing access to data to many within the community.

As stated above, indicators are not new. What is new about the current use of indicators is:

- typically more citizen involvement or representation of citizens in the process of identifying and developing specific indicators;

- greater understanding of the need for the integration of indicators into overall planning and development efforts; and

- better reflection of the desires, goals, and visions that the community aims to achieve over the long term.

Planners, officials, and citizens, in particular, need to clearly understand this last point. Change on a communitywide scale is a long-term process: "creating an initial report card (indicators project) to measure your progress

Indicators don't guarantee results. But results are impossible without proper indicators. And proper indicators, in themselves, can produce results.

—Donella Meadows (1998, 76)

toward becoming a healthy community can take a few months, but realizing the vision may take a generation" (Redefining Progress 1997, 9).

Planners have another reason for incorporating community indicators into their work: community indicators projects or systems represent one way to consistently monitor and evaluate the outcomes of planning policy and action (Murtagh 1998; Seasons 2001). Although monitoring and evaluation have long been recognized as important components in the planning process, the formal means to do that monitoring and evaluation have been absent or used inconsistently. Consequently, planners have sometimes been uncertain "about the efficiency, effectiveness, or impact of their interventions" (Seasons 2001, 2) because of the lack of information to establish causality between interventions and end results. While community indicators projects cannot pretend to establish causality or model community systems, they can provide insight into the connections between actions and outcomes. (See the sidebar for an example from Larimer County, Colorado.)

Community indicators projects or systems represent one way to consistently monitor and evaluate the outcomes of planning policy and action.

LARIMER COUNTY, COLORADO: INDICATORS TO MONITOR AND EVALUATE A COMPREHENSIVE PLAN REVISION

Larimer County, Colorado, embarked on a community indicators project after revision of its 1997 Comprehensive Plan. The revision called for development of an evaluation system to monitor progress toward the plan's new goals. Jill Bennett (2002) of the Larimer County Planning Department explained that the project's purpose has been:

- to provide information to the county's planning commission regarding progress towards achieving the goals and actions of the comprehensive plan;

- to assist the planning and other city staff in decision making and direction; and

- to provide county citizens with the information to hold government accountable to achieve the desired goals and actions of the comprehensive plan.

But if community indicators are so valuable, why are they not fully incorporated into every aspect of planning, particularly in some of planning's most commonly used tools— comprehensive plans and zoning ordinances? There are, admittedly, few examples where community indicators projects have elicited direct, consistent changes within the planning policy and regulatory framework of a community. This lack of effect is often cited by critics of community indicators. But communities that are considering the use of indicators should not be scared off by such critiques. They should instead be prepared to answer questions such as: What happens after the initial interest and participation in indicators and the indicator process? Are positive changes really occurring because a set of indicators now exists for a community? Communities should also keep in mind—and make clear to their citizens—that indicators projects do not represent the whole spectrum of planning but rather represent a more limited process. An indicators project may be used to set boundaries and targets for planning activity, as reflected in visioning activities and goal setting, but the planning activity is often independent. When specific plans and actions are chosen, the indicator priorities may or may not match the planning structure in place.

The assertion in this PAS Report is that community indicators projects should be viewed as tools that can assist planners and planning activities. By integrating the indicators process and resulting goals and objectives of that process, planners will be able to better address community needs and desires. Not all communities or planners will view community indicators projects as positive; however, as reviews of literature and this author's research in the United States and Canada demonstrate, the prevailing view today is that indicators projects are a valuable undertaking.

During my analysis of several western Canadian cities that have community indicators projects, representatives from nonprofit organizations that initiated or participated heavily in these projects expressed their view that the process and the responses elicited by the design and use of indicators were very positive. The most important of these positive outcomes are the general public's increased awareness of community issues and its deeper involvement in decisions about what issues are important to the community. Yet, public-sector planners directly involved with these community indicators projects have also expressed concern that the indicators are not being routinely or fully integrated into comprehensive plans and other major planning activities.

Achieving Change with Indicators

So how does one take a community indicators project to the next stage? In particular, how can indicators specify the actions a community needs to take in order to respond to the problems the indicators have identified? The implications of these questions run deep: planners may have to consider making changes to comprehensive planning and to the implementation of those plans through regulatory devices as well as recommendations to other public agencies about the capital improvements budget and even tax and fiscal policy. In other words, this is the realm in which community indicators are tested. Only successful indicators will affect policy outcomes in the public sector.

Criticism of community indicators often focuses on the lack of scientifically proven models to identify, design, and test them. Some researchers propose that indicators, in order to be successful, should take an approach that uses an analytic method

> that looks for causal relationships between events rather than simply at the events themselves. The success of this approach has been based on the development of models and hypotheses about how the world works. The purpose of indicators is then to help develop and test the validity of the models. If the indicators chosen illustrate the validity of a theory, then the indicators project has a handle on solving real problems. (Cobb and Rixford 1998, 31)

But this analytic method seems to be a particularly large stretch for indicators because testing the validity of models does not appear to be the objective of most indicators projects. Today, successful projects more often use a bottom-up, qualitative research approach in which local observations and analysis give rise to a multiplicity of theories appropriate only in specific contexts.

Some planners now also consider community indicators projects as proactive tools, not reactive records: these projects can be precursors to change and tools used to create positive effects. Thomas Kingsley, in his work with 19 community indicators projects, supports this view. He believes that the most exciting thing about indicators is that they move people off dead center—new information is brought to bear so people can act now and come together (Kingsley 2002). Planners know how difficult this prompt to action and "coming together" can be, emphasizing once again the value of indicators for land-use planning and citizen involvement.

Even though this perspective is gaining more support, problems exist with using indicators as precursors of change. A recent study of planners in 14 municipalities in Ontario (Seasons 2001) revealed that, despite the

WHY PLANNERS SHOULD USE INDICATORS

1. Indicators democratize information, ideally leading to positive change through community activisim by many constituencies.

2. Indicators can embody the inherent values of a community, encouraging public sector responses that reflect these values. Likewise, working towards common goals can reduce conflict in communities.

3. Indicators represent a method to gauge accurately the economic, environmental, and social conditions within a community over the long term, allowing for more effective and informed decision making.

4. Indicators systems or projects, when effectively designed and implemented, can improve evaluation of planning policy and actions by helping establish causality between planning interventions and outcomes.

plethora of information available about indicators, their use was constricted by a variety of factors. For example:

- models may be too complex and expensive to design and maintain;

- indicators may be viewed with suspicion in jurisdictions that rely on ad hoc and other more flexible decision-making methods;

- robust, effective indicators can be difficult to develop;

- previous dissatisfaction with indicators; and

- a lack of resources or incentives to research and design indicators (p. 9).

The perception that models may be too expensive or complex can be overcome by examining applications from other communities. Indeed, the initial start-up process and data gathering can be daunting, but can be mitigated if conducted in the context of a collaborative effort. The remaining four factors are related. In other words, planners and citizens may not see the immediate application of indicators. The use of indicators may be difficult to integrate into current plans and processes, although these constraining factors can be overcome as well. It is vital to recognize that indicators are tools, not the end results, and planning outcomes cannot necessarily be directly measured by indicators. If indicators are viewed as a way to *assist* in the planning process, rather than representing what in some cases may be unobtainable goals, planners may not be constrained in their use.

Emerging Developments

While the debates over and study of the best approach to community indicators continue, there are numerous examples of exciting emerging developments. One of these, integrated assessment modeling, holds particular promise: it may allow communities to fully integrate indicators into the public policy process. This full integration is what many communities are seeking and can be considered the next stage of community indicators.

Integrated assessment modeling, when used as a city planning tool, is defined as the assessment of the sociocultural, economic, and environmental characteristics of a community and the specific identification of the mutual dependence of planning and societal trends at the strategic and operational level (Van Asselt et al. 2001; Rijkens-Klomp et al. 2000). With the goal of generating

SUMMARY OF CONDITION INDICATORS AVAILABLE IN SEATT	
Transportation	**Environmental**
Commute patterns: non-single-occupant-vehicle commute trips (EAA and CP)	Air quality (EAA and CP)
	Canopy/tree coverage (EAA and CP)
Transit ridership (EAA and CP)	Energy consumption (EAA and CP)
Alternative transportation facilities (EAA and CP)	Open space (EAA and CP)
	Stream water quality (EAA and CP)
Motor vehicle injuries and deaths (CC and EAA)	Water consumption (EAA and CP)
Safety and equity (EAA)	Salmon populations (EAA)
Regional greenhouse gas emissions (EAA)	Residents' environmental eth (EAA)
Transportation Demand Management programs (EAA)	Residents' environmental stewardship activities (EAA)
Mobility (EAA)	Recycling rates (CP)
	Noise levels (CP)
Ease of access to shops and services (CC)	Pollution in neighborhoods (CC

(CP) Comprehensive Plan Progress Rep

22

frameworks that organize knowledge to enable study of complex social issues, integrated assessment modeling combines various pieces of disciplinary science so as to support decision making (ICIS 1999, 4).

Organizations such as the United Nations and the International Institute for Sustainable Development have developed training programs incorporating some of these frameworks for environmental assessment and reporting. Often using regions as their focus, these training sessions, held throughout the world, encourage the use of integrated assessment models to increase accountability and uncover the interaction of environmental trends with economic and social policies (Swanson 2002). The underlying appeal for planners of integrative assessment is that it adds a "fourth" dimension to the environmental-economic-social triangle by focusing on how institutional/governmental interaction is vital. An integrated assessment model is currently under development for the city of Maastricht in the Netherlands (see Van Asselt et al. 2001; Rijkens-Klomp et al. 2000).

Beyond developing new methodologies, other communities are more tightly integrating community indicators with local governments' decision-making processes. The initial results are encouraging. For example, Seattle has established an Office of Sustainability and Environment (OSE), one of the first offices of its kind in the United States. Located in

ealth	Social	Economic
tress (CC)	Population by race (CP)	Population, number of households, employment, growth targets (CP)
obacco and alcohol se (CC)	Feeling safe in neighborhoods (CC and CP)	Household income (CP)
hysical activity (CC)	Crime levels (CC and CP)	
	Family violence (CC)	Income distribution (CC and CP)
hysical activity and eight (CC)	Households with children (CP)	
	High school dropout rate (CP)	Livable wage income (CC)
nfant mortality (CC)	Education level of population (CP)	
estricted activity due to nysical/mental health C)	Teen births (CC and CP)	Persons below poverty level (CC and CP)
	Freedom from discrimination (CC)	
	Health insurance coverage and access (CC and CP)	Adequate food (CC)
	Social support (CC)	Low-income-housing units (CP)
	Positive social values and behavior in youth (CC)	
	Neighborhood social cohesion (CC)	Housing affordability (CC and CP)
	Institutional support for community service (CC)	
	Volunteering (CP)	Home ownership (CP)
	Participation in life-enriching activities (CC)	Family-friendly employee benefits (CC)
	Involvement in community organizations (CC)	
	Parent/guidance involvement in children's learning (CC)	
	Quality, affordable childcare (CC)	
	Developmental assets, risk and protective factors in youth (CC)	
	Academic achievement (CC)	

C) Communities Count Indicators   (EAA) Environmental Action Agenda Measures

Source: Office of Sustainability and Environment, City of Seattle, Washington, October, 2002.

the mayor's office, OSE works closely with city departments and elected officials to elicit changes in public programs and policies to be more consistent with sustainable development goals like those in the Condition Indicators set (see sidebar on pages 22 and 23). Three interrelated missions drive the OSE:

1. Implement the Environmental Management Plan to reduce impacts of city facilities, operations, and services.

2. Evaluate and integrate long-term economic, environmental, and social considerations into city plans, actions, and expenditures to form a sustainability management system with a "triple bottom line" of economic prosperity, environmental quality, and social justice.

3. Identify and pursue opportunities to accelerate the adoption of sustainable development practices throughout the community and region. (Seattle OSE 2001, 5)

Broad representation often brings together those who otherwise may not have constructive opportunities to engage in dialogue about community goals.

Within the Austin, Texas, Transportation, Planning and Sustainability Department, the staff of the Sustainable Communities Initiative (SCI) has developed a system for gauging whether capital improvement projects are consistent with sustainable development goals and the community's set of indicators. Using the CIP Sustainability Matrix, staff rate alternative actions assigning values and weighted values to each choice (SCI 2002). The results are then used as an aid in decision making about policy changes and program activities.

Integrating Community Indicators With Planning

The indicators process varies from community to community, yet, after studying community indicator projects since the 1990s, Redefining Progress specified 10 steps commonly used to identify, develop, and integrate a set of indicators. (See Figure 2.)

The first step for any community, according to Redefining Progress, is to form a working group. This group provides a community with the opportunity to bring together diverse organizations that reflect its needs and desires. Many community indicators projects have representation from the public, private, and nonprofit sectors of the community. This broad representation often brings together those who otherwise may not have constructive opportunities to engage in dialogue about community goals. Indeed, by the time the group progresses to the third step—identifying the community's shared values and vision—its members may have already realized that, despite significant differences in their approaches, their desired outcomes are the same.

But before the group reaches this understanding, the second step calls for clarification of purpose, one of the most important aspects of designing an indicators project. As Redefining Progress explains, indicators are most effective when directed to a specific purpose. This purpose typically falls into one of three categories:

1. *Public education* that introduces a set of values or ideas and mobilizes response and action

2. *Policy background* information is provided to aid in the policy decision-making process

3. *Performance evaluation*, in which indicators are used to establish benchmarks to measure the achievement of goals (Redefining Progress 1997, 13).

FIGURE 2. INDICATOR PROCESS

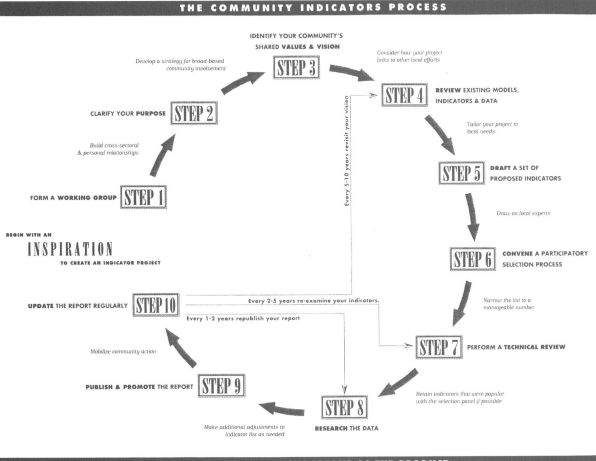

THE COMMUNITY INDICATORS PROCESS

IDENTIFY YOUR COMMUNITY'S SHARED **VALUES & VISION**

Develop a strategy for broad-based community involvement

STEP 3

Consider how your project links to other local efforts

STEP 4 **REVIEW** EXISTING MODELS, INDICATORS & DATA

CLARIFY YOUR **PURPOSE** **STEP 2**

Tailor your project to local needs

Build cross-sectoral & personal relationships

STEP 5 **DRAFT** A SET OF PROPOSED INDICATORS

FORM A **WORKING GROUP** **STEP 1**

Every 5-10 years revisit your vision

Draw on local experts

BEGIN WITH AN

INSPIRATION

TO CREATE AN INDICATOR PROJECT

STEP 6 **CONVENE** A PARTICIPATORY SELECTION PROCESS

UPDATE THE REPORT REGULARLY **STEP 10**

Every 2-5 years re-examine your indicators.

Narrow the list to a manageable number

Every 1-2 years republish your report

Mobilize community action

STEP 7 PERFORM A **TECHNICAL REVIEW**

PUBLISH & PROMOTE THE REPORT **STEP 9**

Retain indicators that were popular with the selection panel if possible

STEP 8

Make additional adjustments to indicator list as needed

RESEARCH THE DATA

THE PROCESS IS AS IMPORTANT AS THE PRODUCT

The indicators process is a long-term one. Just as with most types of planning, its scope and breadth requires a far-sighted and far-reaching timeline. Estimates of the time it takes to design and conduct an initial indicators project range from several months to more than two years. Once the initial project is completed, updates can be periodic or ongoing, as in the case of Jacksonville, Florida, program, which began in 1974 and continues indefinitely.

Shorter projects can be very focused, designed to identify a core set of indicators (typically, somewhere between 20 and 50 indicators comprise the set) and to act upon them (e.g., adopting several indicators into a community's comprehensive plan). Even if the process to establish the indicators is relatively short, realize that the community indicators projects must persist to be effective: an indicators project must exist long enough to establish the time-series of data necessary to monitor community change.

Yet these projects must also evolve over time: planners and other officials must always refine and improve their data-collection methods and be ready to revise the project's aims so as to accommodate social or economic change (Redefining Progress 1997).

Although its benefits to the community can far outweigh its costs, an indicators project can be expensive and time consuming. Many governments have found that partnering with other governments or with non-governmental organizations—or even developing a separate body (such

Shorter projects can be very focused, designed to identify a core set of indicators.

as a nonprofit organization)—can ensure that adequate attention is paid to an indicator project process and that the costs of the process are more widely distributed. A government partnership with a nongovernmental organization is perhaps the most common approach taken to indicators projects: typically, the nongovernmental organization initiates the project and may receive financial and other support from the local or regional government. Many of these projects build community participation into the indicator development process—either through forums, surveys, interviews, or other means of gaining citizen input. Often, an oversight team will be selected that includes representatives from the community and government sectors, including planners.

Hazards Planners Should Avoid

While the science of indicators projects has not been perfected, benefits still accrue to those communities and planners willing to use them. Yet several significant problems continue to plague these projects. Identifying feasible and valid indicators is perhaps the biggest problem. Donella Meadows (1998, 4) specified seven hazards to avoid in the indicator identification and selection process:

1. Overconfidence: faulty indicators can lead to wrong decisions.

2. Incompleteness: despite their usefulness, indicators do not completely represent reality because they cannot reflect the many subtleties and other attributes of the "real" system.

3. Dependence on a false model: do the indicators show what is desirable or actually happening?

4. Measuring what is measurable rather than what is important: data that simply can be measured should not obscure what is really needed, as determined by the community.

5. Over-aggregation: too much data grouped together distorts the measurement.

6. Deliberate falsification: data should not be altered or delayed if considered negative.

7. Diverting attention from direct experience: indicators may obscure real experiences, especially if the numbers based on indicators are positive.

Development of useful indicators can also be derailed by conflicts over who should be responsible for their development.

Development of useful indicators can also be derailed by conflicts over who should be responsible for their development. Planners already use fundamental indicators, such as traffic counts, so the newfound emphasis by others on indicators may prompt planners to feel that they are "under siege with advice on how to do planning" (Maser 2002). This is an important issue for planners: Are indicators another way to "blame planners" when growth issues arise, for example? If desired indicator levels in certain measurement areas are not met, do planners and planning activities become the focus of discontent?

Yet indicator projects can provide planners with an opportunity to foster greater cooperation between themselves and others. With their unique skills, planners can educate others on how indicators as a tool can aid the planning process but should not be viewed as the overriding factor in making decisions. In other words, planners can explain that the planning process is complex and interrelated with other facets of the community and that, by taking indicators into account, the planning process can be enhanced.

This need for accepting and using indicators in the planning process is still very much in the evolutionary stage; there are, in fact, very few examples where planners in local government have initiated an indicators project. Rather, other divisions of government or nonprofit groups remain the primary initiators.

IDENTIFYING AND SELECTING INDICATORS FOR COMMUNITY DEVELOPMENT: CASE STUDIES

There are two principal methods for indicator identification and selection.

The first is a top-down approach in which experts define the set of indicators a project will use. This approach is common for national and international programs. The advantage in those cases is that "pre-defined" measurement tools can be used by a wide range of different organizations, allowing for more homogenous, scientifically valid sets of indicators. However, this approach may lack a sense of community priorities (Hardi et al. 1997, 75).

The second approach, and the more common at the local level in the United States, is a bottom-up approach in which indicators are initiated and identified through a participatory process typically involving citizens, community leaders, and perhaps independent consultants. This approach allows the community to become more vested in the process, but it risks being too narrowly focused, thus overlooking larger issues such as sustainable development across a region (Hardi et al. 1997, 75–76). Indeed, regional approaches continue to be an area in which much work needs to be done. One only has to look at the idea of sustainability to see the need to incorporate a regional approach: how can one community develop indicators aimed at improving, for example, air quality, something affected by many communities throughout a region?

Some indicators projects use a hybrid approach, using standards established in a top-down approach but allowing for more input at the local level. An example is the indicators monitoring system for the Federation of Canadian Municipalities (FCM) Quality of Life Reporting System. This group, with 1,035 participating member municipalities across Canada, encourages the use of indicators for the development of public policy. Its reporting system includes both "subjective-qualitative indicators such as 'sense of community' and objective-quantitative indicators like 'number of monument sites'" (ICSC 2001, 27; see also FCM 2003). FCM uses three primary criteria when selecting indicators:

1. Variables must be meaningful at the community level.

2. Data must be consistently (at least annually) available at a national level.

3. Variables must be easily understood by the public (ICSC 2001, 27).

By interweaving indicators that both address community interests and use national data, FCM's criteria represent a successful hybrid approach.

Whether top-down, bottom-up, or hybrid, the indicator selection process usually moves through three major stages: preparatory, development, and institutionalization (Hardi and Pinter 1995). This process is illustrated in Figure 3. During the preparatory stage, criteria for indicator selection are determined and issue areas are selected. The central feature of the development stage is achieving consensus on crucial issues and includes selection, linking, and target-setting activities. The level of citizen involvement in building this consensus will vary during this stage, depending on the approach taken. Finally, during the institutionalization stage, the indicators, plans for review, and allocation of resources are approved by legislative or organizational authorities.

Some indicators projects use a hybrid approach, using standards established in a top-down approach but allowing for more input at the local level.

FIGURE 3. THE THREE STAGES OF INDICATOR SELECTION

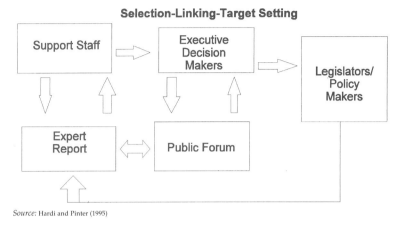

Source: Hardi and Pinter (1995)

A comprehensive set of indicators has been built on the work begun in 1994 and are now reflected in the Santa Monica Sustainable City Plan.

It is this third and final stage where integration with planning and development activities can be achieved. Unless public sector agencies endorse and use the indicator set, changes in policy and programs will not result. As discussed above, one of the major reasons for the failure of earlier indicators projects was a failure to integrate indicators into public policy and implementation after the indicators were identified.

Santa Monica, California

One community that has made progress in its efforts to integrate indicators into overall community development is Santa Monica, California. In 1994, its city council adopted the Santa Monica Sustainable Development Program to implement the city's existing and planned sustainability programs (Besleme 1999, 2). The effort began with volunteers working with city staff to identify specific targets in four policy areas: resource conservation, transportation, pollution prevention and public health protection, and community and economic development. Sixteen indicators, each relating to principles and defining major goals, were identified and have been monitored since 1994; four more have been added since that time. Targets have been established, and semi-annual reviews gauge progress.

The city has had success on several fronts, including the conversion to "green" electricity derived from nearby geothermal sources for most city facilities and a plan to increase the use of reduced-emissions fuel in city fleet vehicles (Commonwealth Energy 1999).

These achievements rose directly from concern expressed in the indicators. For example, one indicator showed that only 15 percent of the municipal fleet vehicles used reduced-emissions fuel; in response, the city instituted a plan to increase use to 75 percent by 2000, using this indicator to monitor and change its own behavior (Cobb and Rixford 1998; Besleme 1999). The city was able to meet a 70 percent goal by 2000 and a 75 percent goal attainment in 2002 (Kubani 2003).

A comprehensive set of indicators has been built on the work begun in 1994 and are now reflected in the Santa Monica Sustainable City Plan. This plan has eight goal areas, with specific goals reflected within each area. The eight areas are:

- Resource Conservation

- Environmental and Public Health

- Transportation

- Economic Development

- Open Space and Land Use

- Housing

- Community Education and Civic Participation

- Human Dignity (Santa Monica 2003)

Table 3 provides a matrix listing Santa Monica's indicators and goals.

Even though Santa Monica's planning department was not the initiator of the indicators project, it participates by virtue of the fact that California statutes require comprehensive plans to include a conservation element. This requirement, combined with strong community interest in sustainable development issues, has prompted Santa Monica to integrate the indicators across a variety of planning contexts. As Dean Kubani (2002), director of the city's environmental programs division, explained,

> Since many of the overarching goals reflected in the set of indicators relate to how we plan our communities, planning is a natural fit. While not driven by the planning department, indicators are becoming integrated into planning regulations and activities. For example, our Green Building Design and Construction Standards for any development over three units have to comply with our guidelines and specific ordinances. This program is managed by the Planning Department.

In a speech to the Mayors' Asia-Pacific Environmental Summit, the mayor of Santa Monica, Pam O'Connor (1999), told participants that the city has learned several lessons from the indicators project:

- "Adopting measurable targets creates accountability and overcomes inertia."

- "It's necessary to perform regular and rigorous evaluation of targets, and it is sometimes necessary to modify indicators and targets."

- "We learned the importance of emphasizing [the] overall cost-effectiveness of sustainability programs to demonstrate their direct link to a healthy local economy."

Truckee Meadows, Nevada

Like Santa Monica, the Truckee Meadows Regional Planning Agency (TMRPA)—which oversees southern Washoe County and the cities of Sparks and Reno in Nevada—has also undertaken a comprehensive community indicators project. It was initiated when indicators were made one of the policy mandates of the local governments' 1991 Regional Plan, as required by state law. The TMRPA was given responsibility for its implementation. At the same time, a nonprofit community-based organization, Truckee Meadows Tomorrow (TMT), was created to promote public consensus on the concept of quality of life so as to further economic development efforts (Besleme et al. 1999).

TMRPA, together with TMT, formed a task force and steering committee of representatives drawn from the region's local governments and communities to oversee the process. The data gathering and compilation was carried out by TMRPA staff and volunteers, while promotional events and related activities were conducted by TMT. Based on a quality-of-life framework, the project's primary goal was to mediate growth conflicts. Citizen participation was instrumental to the process: 3,000 citizen surveys were completed, and 100 citizen volunteers served on a Quality of Life Task Force (Besleme et al. 1999).

Since many of the overarching goals reflected in the set of indicators relate to how we plan our communities, planning is a natural fit.
—DEAN KUBANI (2002)

TABLE 3
SANTA MONICA SUSTAINABLE CITY PLAN
GOAL/INDICATOR MATRIX

The matrix below lists all of the Sustainable City indicators in the leftmost column and the eight Sustainable City goal areas across the top. For each indicator, dots are shown for every goal area about which the indicator provides information. While each indicator was developed to measure progress toward meeting goals in one goal area, this matrix shows that many of the indicators measure the conditions, impacts, or effectiveness of actions in several goal areas. This demonstrates the linkages between each of the goal areas and the impact of decisions across environmental, economic, and social boundaries.

	Resource Conservation	Environmental and Public Health	Transportation	Economic Development	Open Space and Land Use	Housing	Community Education and Civic Participation	Human Dignity
Resource Conservation Indicators								
Solid waste generation	●			●				
Water use	●	●		●			●	
Energy use	●	●	●	●		●		
Renewable energy use	●	●		●			●	
Greenhouse gas emissions	●	●	●	●	●	●		
Ecological footprint for Santa Monica	●	●	●	●	●	●		
Indicator of sustainable procurement	●	●		●				
"Green" construction	●	●	●			●		
Environmental and Public Health Indicators								
Santa Monica Bay beach closures		●		●	●			
Wastewater (sewage) generation	●	●						
Vehicle miles traveled	●	●	●	●	●	●		
Air quality	●	●	●					
Residential household hazardous waste		●						
City purchases of hazardous materials		●						
Toxic air contaminant releases		●						
Urban runoff reduction	●	●	●		●			
Fresh, local, organic produce		●	●	●				
Organic produce—Farmer's markets		●	●	●				
Restaurant produce purchases		●	●	●				
Food choices	●	●	●	●				
Transportation Indicators								
Modal split	●	●	●			●		
Residential use of sustainable trans. options	●	●	●			●		●
Sufficiency of transportation options			●					
Bicycle lanes and paths			●			●		
Vehicle ownership	●	●	●	●				
Bus ridership	●	●	●					
Alternative fueled vehicles—city fleet	●	●	●					
Traffic congestion			●		●	●		
Pedestrian and bicycle safety			●					
Traffic impacts to emergency response			●		●	●		

(continued)

	Resource Conservation	Environmental and Public Health	Transportation	Economic Development	Open Space and Land Use	Housing	Community Education and Civic Participation	Human Dignity
Economic Development Indicators								
Economic diversity				●				
Business reinvestment in the community				●			●	
Jobs/Housing balance			●	●		●		●
Cost of living				●		●		●
Quality job creation				●				●
Income disparity				●				●
Resource efficiency of local businesses	●	●		●				
Local employment of city staff			●	●		●		
Open Space and Land Use Indicators								
Open space		●			●			
Trees	●	●			●			
Parks accessibility			●		●	●	●	
Land use and development			●		●	●		
Regionally appropriate vegetation	●				●			
Housing Indicators								
Availability of affordable housing				●		●		●
Distribution of affordable housing				●	●	●		●
Affordable housing for special needs groups						●		●
Production of "livable" housing	●		●	●	●	●		
Production of "green" housing	●	●				●		
Community Education and Civic Participation Indicators								
Voter participation							●	
Participation in civic affairs							●	
Empowerment							●	●
Community involvement							●	
Volunteering							●	
Participation in neighborhood organizations							●	
Sustainable community involvement 1	●	●	●		●			
Sustainable community involvement 2	●	●	●	●	●	●	●	●
Human Dignity Indicators								
Basic needs—shelter						●		●
Basic needs—health Care								●
Basic needs—economic opportunity				●				●
Basic needs—public safety								●
Residents' perception of safety								●
Incidents of abuse								●
Incidents of discrimination				●		●		●
Education/Youth								●
Empowerment				●				●
Ability to meet basic needs				●	●	●		●

Source: City of Santa Monica (2003)

To institutionalize the indicators, the TMRPA planning commission developed a monitoring process intended to analyze the indicators to see if critical aspects of quality of life were changing, and if so, whether for better or worse. The process required that, if the region were unable to maintain its desired quality of life as measured and defined by indicators, the annual and five-year reviews of the Regional Plan would include considerations of stricter policies or programs to address those areas where the region had fallen short. These stricter policies would be based on lowered population projections and, if necessary, conditions that limited development projects (Besleme et al. 1999, 25).

This approach let the region avoid either a no-growth or pro-growth stance; the TMRPA instead chose to promote a middle ground of quality growth (Besleme et al. 1999). This "middle-ground" is reminiscent of the type of planning advocated by Martin Meyerson (1956, 59), who described it as an intermediate set of planning functions performed on an ongoing basis. He identified middle-ground planning functions that included a pulse-taking function to "alert the community through quarterly or other periodic reports to danger signs in blight formation, in economic changes, population movements and other shifts" as well as a feedback review function to gauge the consequences of program and project activities as guides to actions (Meyerson 1956, 60). In other words, there may be ways to accomplish desirable planning and development outcomes other than relying too heavily on regulatory aspects—to meet in the middle or on terms that can be agreeable to the parties involved.

TMRPA's project has produced concrete results. One of the project's indicators showed that lower-income households in the region were spending a disproportionately high share of their incomes on housing. TMRPA responded by establishing a goal to increase affordable housing options. The agency then provided training in tax-exempt bond financing to public agencies and private developers; the result was more than 700 new affordable housing units built between 1995 and 1999 (Besleme 1999). While the TMPRA can't claim their efforts alone were responsible for this growth, the agency feels strongly that, by changing regulations and encouraging incentives for developers, affordable housing became a reality.

Vancouver, British Columbia

The International Center for Sustainable Cities has been working since the late 1990s with local planners and others in the Greater Vancouver Regional District to further develop the concept of "complete communities" as one of four major directions outlined in the district's Livable Region Strategic Plan (Seymoar et al. 2001). The other three directions are protecting the green zone, achieving a compact metropolitan region, and increasing transportation choices (Greater Vancouver Regional District 2001). Indicators are being developed as a monitoring tool for assessing progress toward the broad goals identified as part of the complete communities approach. These goals include seeking a better balance in jobs and labor force locations throughout the region; seeking a diversity of housing options; and seeking development of a network of high-quality, mixed-use urban centers. During its indicator development process, the Vancouver Regional District moved from general interests to a specific goal and then to indicators. As seen in Table 4, for example, indicators can describe at a high level of specificity the desire of residents to meet daily needs locally, which is one component of the district's complete community concept.

In other words, there may be ways to accomplish desirable planning and development outcomes other than relying too heavily on regulatory aspects.

TABLE 4
COMPLETE COMMUNITIES EXAMPLE OF PROXY INDICATORS

Broad Component/Desire	Goal	Proxy Indicators
Daily Needs of Citizens Met Locally	Compact, Mixed-Use, Accessible Urban Centers to Allow for Day-to-Day Needs to be Met Locally	❑ Land-use patterns accommodate a mix of uses (i.e., residential, commercial, institutional, recreational, cultural, social, etc.)
		❑ Land-use patterns promote walking, biking, and transit access to employment, education, recreation, entertainment, retail, services, etc.
		❑ Efficient use of land (infill, brownfields redevelopment, densification)
		❑ Urban centers appropriately scaled to community (i.e., region, municipal/town, community/area, neighborhood)
		❑ Neighborhood centers contain local businesses that serve daily needs of nearby residents

Source: Seymoar et al. (2001)

Winnipeg, Manitoba

Winnipeg, Manitoba, has established a three-tier planning framework to integrate long-term plans and day-to-day activities using an indicators system. Gerry Couture (2000), a planner with the city, described the system:

> Our first tier is the community level, using indicators as the proxy for what is desired by the citizens. The second tier is the corporate level, for looking at the city as a service provider. And the third tier is the [city] departmental-level service provision. The system is subjective but we try to relate community-level indicators to service and performance measures. Although direct correlation is difficult, the system provides us with measures of satisfaction that we can use.

As Winnipeg's system shows, the process of integrating and opening up lines of communication often has the most value in indicators projects. Improved communication among city departments as well as between city departments and citizens and businesses/organizations in the community has increased awareness of planning and what is required to tie indicators to specific measures.

Palm Beach County, Florida: A Rural Application

Rural areas are particularly challenged when faced with designing and implementing community indicators systems. As mentioned above, rural communities typically face one of two problems: rural communities may be suffering from economic decline and thus want to stabilize and improve economic conditions, or they may be experiencing growth pressures from adjacent urban areas.

The case of the Central Western Communities (CWC) of Palm Beach County, Florida, falls in the second category. A rural district in an unincorporated section of the county, the CWC covers 57,500 acres, of which 30

Rural areas are particularly challenged when faced with designing and implementing community indicators systems.

percent is in agricultural use. Another 6,609 acres are in conservation use or are otherwise open protected lands. Traditionally an area of citrus production, rural farms, and small communities, this area is quickly being consumed by encroaching urban growth. Existing communities in the CWC are comprised predominately of single-family homes or lots.

Beginning in 1999, Palm Beach County government developed its Optional Sector Plan for the CWC, which focused on:

- creating sustainable growth;

- preserving regionally significant natural resources;

- coordinating services and facilities;

- determining the community's physical form;

- generating economic development; and

- timing and phasing development.

Gene Boles, a planner with the University of Florida's Community Outreach Program who participated in the sector plan study, said the county's priority was preservation of the area's rural identity. "Palm Beach County is an urban county, but the remaining rural communities in the CWC desire to retain their rural character," he said. "It's important to protect these areas in terms of not only environmental outcomes but social and economic outcomes as well" (Boles 2002). Working with a private consulting firm, WilsonMiller, the county embarked on a five-stage planning process:

Stage 1: Community Profile

Stage 2: Visioning and Alternative Futures Analysis

Stage 3: Plan Formulation

Stage 4: Implementation Tools

Stage 5: Adoption (WilsonMiller 2002)

As part of Stage 2, a set of indicators was constructed to guide subsequent decision making. The county and WilsonMiller established guiding principles for the indicator selection process based on community priorities that were identified through residents' participation in a series of public forums. These guiding principles were then assigned a value or weight, and these values in turn were used to select a set of indicators. According to a WilsonMiller (2002, 43) report,

> The assignment of weighted value is straightforward. A total of 100 points is available and these points may be assigned to the Guiding Principles as the evaluator sees fit. The relative importance of the Guiding Principles reflects the stated mission of the CWC Sector Plan, interpretation of the Palm Beach County Comprehensive Plan, and perceptions of community values from public review and input.

The values in Table 5 reflect the planning and development priorities of the CWC.

Those indicators measuring preservation of rural character and conservation of open space were thus most likely to be selected for the county's sector plan. The county adopted, for example, four indicators associated with this principle:

1. Population growth, measured as the percentage change from existing conditions

"It's important to protect these areas in terms of not only environmental outcomes but social and economic outcomes as well."
—GENE BOLES (2002)

TABLE 5
PALM BEACH COUNTY, FLORIDA
PLANNING AND DEVELOPMENT PRIORITIES

Guiding Principles	Value
Preserve Rural Character/Conserve Open Space	30
Promote Sustainable and Livable Communities	20
Promote Environmental Sustainability	15
Manage Water Resources	15
Provide Adequate Services and Facilities	10
Minimize Traffic Impacts	5
Promote Economic Sustainability	5
Composite	**100**

Source: Wilson Miller (2002, 43)

2. Gross density, measured as dwelling units per gross acre

3. Agriculture retention, measured as the percentage of existing agriculture acreage retained

4. Open space, measured as acres of open space per dwelling unit

Accordingly, the principles with relatively low priority have fewer associated indicators. In all, the county's sector plan includes 25 indicators that reflect this set of guiding principles. This is a manageable number, yet these indicators are comprehensive enough to record changes in the CWC. The Palm Beach County Planning Department has primary responsibility for monitoring and using the system.

The concept of weighting certain indicators is a valuable tool because it stresses a community's highest priorities. Often, an indicator project will treat each indicator with equal importance and thus overlooks the differing values a community attaches to each. But a numerical weighting system cannot replace careful planning decisions. As the WilsonMiller report (2002, 43) makes clear, this system is only "a tool. It is an aid to the decision-making process, not a substitute. The goal is to allow a comparison of outcomes and to assist in the construction of preferred implementation strategies that meet the Guiding Principles as closely as possible."

The concept of weighting certain indicators is a valuable tool because it stresses a community's highest priorities.

Calgary, Alberta

Sustainable Calgary is a citizen-initiated effort to direct future growth and development outcomes in Calgary, Alberta. Begun in 1996, Sustainable Calgary created the State of Our City Project, an indicators project aimed at assessing sustainability. In 2001, Sustainable Calgary released its second *State of Our City Report*, which documents 36 indicators, selected and researched by almost 2,000 residents of Calgary over four years. The indicators are divided into six categories:

1. Community

2. Economy

3. Education

4. Natural environment

5. Resource use

6. Wellness

According to Noel Keough, the director of Sustainable Calgary, the process of identifying, designing, and monitoring the indicators has been valuable to the community. "While not a lot of policy changes have occurred yet," Keough (2002) said, "the work is cited in local government materials and meetings, so awareness of the issues has increased. It also sends a powerful message that citizens want to direct outcomes, not just accept what may happen."

An interest in directing outcomes suggested by groups like Sustainable Calgary also prompted the city to participate in the Federation of Canadian Municipalities' Quality of Life Reporting System. As described earlier in this report, the FCM system enables monitoring of communities' economic, social, and environmental health and provides opportunities for municipalities throughout Canada to work together on policies and planning systems aimed at improving quality of life (Calgary 2001). The data collected and reflected in the indicator set are nationally consistent, allowing for cross-municipality comparisons.

Additionally, the Calgary Policy and Planning Division has developed its own Indices of Community Well-Being, a set of social indicators that generates data used to compare groups to each other so as "to identify incidence and risk of selected social problems for communities and for particular at-risk groups within the community" (Calgary 2000, 3). Groups are identified on the basis of income (incidence of poverty), ethnicity, and age, among other factors. These indices likewise provide "data on key social and economic indicators to inform program planners and policy makers in the City of Calgary and the community" as well as "measures of well-being of Calgary communities relative to other communities and the city as a whole" (p. 3).

TABLE 6
CALGARY'S INDICES OF WELL-BEING

Dimensions	Indicators	Variables
Economic Well-Being	Poverty	Persons in Low-Income Households
		Children in Supports for Independence (SFI) Households
		Seniors Receiving Guaranteed Income Support (GIS)
	Employment	Unemployed Adults
		Unemployed Youth
Social Well-Being	Family Stability	Lone-Parent Families
	Social Inclusion	Recent Movers
		Recent Immigrants
		Official Language Capacity
		Unattached Individuals
		Seniors Living Alone
	Education	Persons Not Completing High School
	Housing	Renters Spending > 30% of Income on Shelter Costs
		Families Below Housing Affordability Threshold
		Dwellings Requiring Major Repair
Physical Well-Being	Personal Health	Hospital Inpatients
		Emergency Room Visits
	Personal Safety	Personal and Property Crimes

Source: City of Calgary (2000,2)

Indicators are most valuable as a means of communication, said Derek Cook, a policy planner in Calgary's Policy and Planning Division. "It is a way to communicate with the community, in terms they agree upon, as the indicators reflect conditions that most agree need monitoring," Cook (2002) explained. He noted also that the city's indicator set shows clearly its progress toward achieving its goals. Table 6 lists Calgary's Indices of Community Well-Being.

The indices were developed using an evaluative approach that measured differences in social welfare between any two groups of people (e.g., comparisons of low- and high-income elderly populations with younger populations). An Index of Volume (INV) and an Index of Risk (INR) are used to calculate the measurements. INV measures the number of individuals experiencing a particular indicator for a particular community and is compiled by summing the number of indicator experiences in each community and dividing by the number of communities to produce a Calgary average. INR measures the percentage of individuals experiencing a particular indicator for a particular community and is constructed by calculating the percentage of individuals in both the given community and the city as a whole (Calgary 2000, 5). This latter index can help identify concerns about social issues for certain populations in the community (e.g., the city can generate an INR for youth between the ages of 15 and 24 who are unemployed).

SOME FINAL THOUGHTS

Undertaking a community indicators project can be a daunting task for planners, especially given the time and resources necessary for a well-designed and effectively implemented project. Yet the benefits are numerous, not only for a community's residents but also for planners, who will be able to use indicators to make better-informed decisions and to gauge more accurately the outcomes of planning activities. Indicators can provide consistent, regular monitoring, which is an integral but often underemployed component of planning.

An indicators project requires substantial advance work. Planners in communities considering a project should first:

- thoroughly research information about how community indicators programs work, including advice on the process from major organizations (see the resources section at the end of this PAS Report);

- identify several "best practices" communities that have implemented an indicators project;

- consider the potential variety of organizational structures for the project, especially the possibility of partnerships between government and nonprofit organizations that could lead to access to sources of funding in some cases that may not be available to public planning departments;

- begin building wide-ranging support so that *all* members of the community understand how they will benefit from the project; and

- develop realistic expectations about how the information from the indicators project will be used (e.g., Will it be integrated into benchmarking or other evaluative activities?).

Planners are often not the initiators of community indicators projects for the variety of reasons discussed above. But it doesn't have to remain this way—planners are uniquely positioned to help direct the future of communities—and indicators can be integrated into planning activities as a tool to help accomplish desired outcomes.

Indicators can provide consistent, regular monitoring, which is an integral but often underemployed component of planning.

One of the concerns expressed by planners about indicators is that they will be yet another way to measure the shortcomings of planning activities. But planners should recognize the ways in which using indicators can *help* them. Many complaints about the lack of desired planning outcomes can be traced to the propensity of some local governments to issue variances that work against the advice of planners and the guiding principles of comprehensive plans. Tying specific indicators to the comprehensive plan, as is being attempted in the Truckee Meadows planning district, is one way that planners can defend against undesirable variances. As emphasized throughout this report, indicators are representative of what a community wants to measure and, as such, what is important to that community. If variances interfere with obtaining desired outcomes—as represented in the comprehensive plan and in indicators developed to measure progress towards those outcomes—indicators, as an expression of public will and policy, can provide political support to planning goals.

Improvements in Cooperation through Data Sharing

Some communities have found that a comprehensive indicators project involving a wide variety of people and organizations leads to greater long-term cooperation for sharing data. If all involved accept the idea of working towards common goals, data issues are less problematic.

A former project manager for the Truckee Meadows Regional Planning District observed that one of the greatest benefits of the district's indicators project has been the collaborative partnerships between regional and local governments, nonprofit organizations, and citizens that have grown as a result of data sharing. "Information has penetrated the discussions of growth and planning," Elise Maser (2002) said. "Just being able to talk about these issues with other organizations has been tremendously valuable for this area."

With the advent of broadly available computer-based technologies to identify and obtain data down to the parcel level, the issue of data sharing is not as prevalent as it once was. Despite the apparent willingness of some communities to share data and the advent of technologies to help manage data, however, potential problems still remain. Disagreements can arise over sharing costs of data collection, competitive advantages to be derived from data, and the variances in data collection methods between jurisdictions. Collaborative efforts are necessary to identify the sources, obtain access to, and gather the myriad data required for calibrating an indicators project.

Many sources of data used to calibrate indicators are available through national, state, and regional sources. For example, 42 different types of automated administrative data files that are typically available in most cities were identified as part of a study for the U.S. Department of Housing and Urban Development (Kingsley et al. 1997). Other data, particularly qualitative data, require surveys and similar data-gathering techniques. These techniques are not only costly but demand significant time as well. Many communities find that a nonprofit organization serving an oversight function can access data and sources of funding (such as private foundations) to help offset the cost of data collection. These groups can then share the data with public agencies and other organizations for use and integration.

Quantitative Reporting, Mapping, and Evaluation

Indicators are used to generate a variety of information, including reports for citizens, website data, and other types of summaries. Numerous organizations issue annual and semi-annual reports directed toward

Some communities have found that a comprehensive indicators project . . . leads to greater long-term cooperation for sharing data.

different audiences—citizens, governments, or other members of a community—that include the data collected through their indicators. Indicators are often presented in the context of sustainability and may include some relation to the elements of the community's comprehensive plan, such as the number of housing units added during the previous year. Some local and regional governments are finding ways to integrate indicators into overall performance evaluation and monitoring (Ammons 1996; Bjornlund 2000), thereby facilitating the preparation of reports that focus on gauging performances and outcomes. A government, for example, can link indicators to elements of its comprehensive plan: progress on the plan's economic development component might be monitored through an indicator that measures businesses added or lost, or the number of properties added to the historic district might be used to track historic preservation goals.

It is often difficult to rely solely on data, such as bland lists of community indicators, to compel citizens and leaders to take action. Integrating indicators with visual aids, such as maps, graphs, and charts, however, can provide a stimulus that encourages immediate response and action (O'Looney 2000). A geographic information system (GIS) can also be constructed for use with community indicators. Series of layers based on spatial datasets using GIS or mapping software can provide a visual "interface" for presenting community indicator data. One disadvantage to using a GIS interface with community indicators is that the data may not always match the community indicators since only those indicators that can be converted for spatial representation can be used. Some social measures may not readily translate into a geographic context. Yet many indicators can be spatially represented, such as environmental resource indicators, physical infrastructure, and community service facilities.

GIS data has been used at the community and neighborhood level to empower citizens and aid in the decision-making process. Cities such as Springfield, Missouri; Milwaukee, Wisconsin; and Philadelphia, Pennsylvania, have made concerted efforts to use GIS technologies with community and neighborhood development organizations so as to generate social, cultural, ethnic, historic, aesthetic, demographic, and economic data (O'Looney 2000, 138). All in all, a GIS system can be invaluable to a community indicators project: it allows easy identification and better access to data than tables of data without graphical representation. Further, changes in these indicators can be more readily monitored and updated with a GIS system.

TOOLS AND RESOURCES

Preparing for a community indicators project requires the use of tools to research, implement, and evaluate the project. These tools can include websites, kits, models, software applications, and reports. Planners in communities considering an indicators project should survey all available tools and choose those that best suit a community's needs and constraints.

Software Programs

Several software programs are currently available that can aid the development of community indicators. Prices of the software differ; for current pricing, please see the websites noted below. While each has its limitations, these programs can serve as useful starting points on which to build a community's particular set of indicators.

The Sustainable Communnity Indicators Program (SCIP). Environment Canada (www.ec.gc.ca) has created the SCIP website (www.ec.gc.ca/scip-pidd/), which is intended to be "an all-in-one starting point for creating,

A government . . . can link indicators to elements of its comprehensive plan.

selecting, and analyzing reporting indicators." Environment Canada offers a software program integrated with its website to assist goal setting, indicator development, data collection and analysis, and documentation. SCIP software includes a set of core indicators that may be drawn on, or users may choose indicators more applicable to their community. Each indicator has a detailed profile that includes potential data sources. Assistance for users is provided at each step of the process.

INDEX. INDEX is GIS-based planning support software developed by Criterion Planners/Engineers that enables benchmarking of conditions and alternative scenario evaluations (www.crit.com/index/index.html). The INDEX model calculates indicator scores based on existing conditions. It also serves a predictive function by providing indicator scores that would result from proposed plans. Unlike SCIP, INDEX requires knowledge of ArcView and Avenue software. It is used by a variety of organizations, including the Florida Department of Community Affairs' Sustainable Community Network (sustainable.state.fl.us), which provides the software and a template of 26 indicators to each of its members.

QUEST. This software simulates alternative futures so as to encourage citizen input. It is user friendly, providing the feel of a game while encouraging debates and discussion about regional sustainability. QUEST was created by the Sustainable Development Institute at the University of British Columbia (www.sdri.ubc.ca). The Georgian Basin Futures Project (www.basinfutures.net) makes use of the software in its GB-QUEST feature.

Organizations: General Information

Sustainable Communities Network
www.sustainable.org/casestudies/studiesindex.html
This organization tracks communities throughout the United States and the rest of the world that are undertaking indicators initiatives.

Compendium of Sustainable Development Indicator Initiatives
iisd1.iisd.ca/measure/compindex.asp
A comprehensive site jointly sponsored by a number of organizations, it provides information on indicator projects at the international, national, and provincial/state/territorial levels.

CitiesPLUS30
www.icsc.ca/cities30.html
Urban sustainability project for 30 cities sharing tools and experiences to implement long-term plans that integrate environmental, social, and economic well-being. Conducted by the International Centre for Sustainable Cities located in Vancouver, British Columbia.

Coalition for Healthier Cities and Communities in the U.S.
www.hospitalconnect.com/communityhlth/about/history.html
Using a healthy families/communities approach, this coalition has developed the community indicators and progress measures project.

Local Agenda 21
www.iclei.org/iclei/la21.htm
The International Council for Local Environmental Initiatives promotes responses to Agenda 21, the global action plan on sustainable development from the 1992 Rio Earth Summit. ICLEI's LA21 program webpage includes information on planning approaches for sustainability at the local level as well as the results of an international survey of local governments' responses to Agenda 21.

Selected Organizations: Local and Regional

Oregon Benchmarks
www.econ.state.or.us/opb/sitemap.htm
The Oregon Progress Board was created by the state to be the steward of the state's strategic plan. The board's Oregon Benchmarks, a set of progress indicators, are known for their excellent design.

Truckee Meadows Regional Planning Agency and Truckee Meadows Tomorrow
www.quality-of-life.org
This project involved thousands of residents and provides an example of how to integrate identified goals with planning and development policies and activities as measured by indicators.

Jacksonville Community Council Inc.
www.jcci.org
JCCI sells a Quality of Life Project and Replication Kit as well as a Community Agenda Reference document. Located in Jacksonville, Florida, this nonprofit organization was among the first to use quality-of-life indicators.

Sustainable Communities Initiative, Austin, Texas
www.ci.austin.tx.us/sustainable/
This site shows how indicators can be integrated with overall planning and development activities.

Sustainable Seattle
www.sustainableseattle.org
Recognized worldwide for their successful approach to sustainability, Sustainable Seattle is a nonprofit civic forum whose mission is to improve the region's long-term well-being.

Seattle's Office of Sustainability and Environment
www.cityofseattle.net/environment
Provides information on public sector use of indicators.

Cape Cod Center for Sustainability
www.vsn.cape.com/~cccenter/
This nonprofit organization was founded to ameliorate the tensions between growth and no-growth advocates in the Cape Cod region. Its indicators cover economic, environmental, and social concerns.

Healthy Families Partnership
www.hampton.va.us/healthyfamilies
Instituted by Hampton, Virginia, this program has garnered much attention from the media and other communities. While not an indicators program per se, it was formed in response to indicators that showed low community health and demonstrates the effect indicators can have on public policy.

Santa Monica Sustainable City Program
www.santa-monica.org/environment/policy/
This site provides a wealth of information on the design and integration of indicators in the public sector. Copies of the program's annual reports are also available and provide examples of indicator data use.

International Institute for Sustainable Development
www.iisd.org
This research and education organization located in Winnipeg, Manitoba, is internationally recognized for its work in a variety of contexts, including application of indicators for achieving sustainable development. This site includes numerous links to indicator research reports.

National Neighborhood Indicators Partnership
www.urban.org/nnip
This program, a collaborative effort of the Urban Institute and local partners, promotes the use of neighborhood-level information systems in local policy making. This site includes information about its partner cities and is a valuable resource for those communities considering a neighborhood-level indicators project.

Federation of Canadian Municipalities
www.fcm.ca
The Federation has promoted the design and use of indicators by communities throughout Canada. On this site are links to information about these and related projects.

Redefining Progress
www.rprogress.org
Redefining Progress was one of the first organizations in the United States to begin monitoring and researching the reemergence of community indicators. Although the organization is now more focused on its Ecological Footprint and Genuine Progress Indicator projects, its site includes links to community indicator resources. Its Community Indicators Handbook is a valuable resource for planners considering whether to embark on an indicators project.

Rocky Mountain Institute
www.rmi.org
This nonprofit group located in Snowmass, Colorado, is a cutting-edge research organization, with projects focusing on renewable energy sources, natural capitalism, and economic renewal. Information on indicators projects in small and midsize cities is included.

Sustainability Institute
www.sustainabilityinstitute.org
This organization, located in Vermont and founded by Donella Meadows, focuses on whole-systems research; it describes its mission as "using systems thinking and organizational learning tools to help people put the principles of sustainability into practice."

University of Florida, Shimberg Center for Affordable Housing, Community Indicators Database Listserve
This list is an e-mail distribution list of more than 250 persons and organizations in Canada and the United States involved in community indicators. To join, e-mail stroh@ufl.edu with mailing address, and phone and e-mail information.

List of References

Ammons, D. N. 1996. *Municipal Benchmarks: Assessing Local Performance and Establishing Community Standards*. Thousand Oaks, Calif.: Sage Publications.

Andrews, J. H. 1996. "Planning Practice: Going by the Numbers." *Planning*, September, 14–18.

Anielski, Mark. 2001. *The Alberta GPI Blueprint: The Genuine Progress Indicator (GPI) Sustainable Well-Being Accounting System*. Drayton Valley, Alberta: Pembina Institute. Also available at www.bgiedu.org/BGI-PDFs/Alberta%20GPI%20Blueprint.pdf%201.pdf.

Association for Community Health Improvement. 2003. "Healthy Communities and Collaboration Resources." [Accessed August 21]. Available at www.hospitalconnect.com/communityhlth/resources/hlthycommunities.html.

Bennett, Jill. 2002. Planner, Planning Department, Larimer County, Colorado. Telephone interview with author, October 30.

Besleme, Kate. 1999. "Community Indicator Projects that Work: How Five Communities Gauge Progress." [Accessed September 13, 2002]. Available at sustainable.state.fl.us/fdi/fscc/news/world/9901/kate_ind.htm.

Besleme, Kate, Elisa Maser, and Judith Silverstein. 1999. *A Community Indicators Case Study: Addressing the Quality of Life in Two Communities*. San Francisco: Redefining Progress. Also available at www.redefiningprogress.org/publications/pdf/CI_CaseStudy1.pdf.

Besleme, Kate, and Megan Mullin. 1997. "Community Indicators and Healthy Communities." *National Civic Review* 86, no. 1: 43–52.

Blair, John P. 1999. "Quality of Life and Economic Development Policy." *Economic Development Review* 16, no. 1: 50–54.

Bjornlund, Lydia. 2000. *Beyond Data: Current Uses of Comparative Performance Measurement in Local Government*. Washington, D.C.: International City/County Management Association.

Boles, Gene. 2002. Director, Community Outreach Program, University of Florida. Personal interview with author, October 7.

Bossel, Hartmut. 1999. *Indicators for Sustainable Development: Theory, Method, Applications*. Winnipeg, Manitoba: International Institute for Sustainable Development. Also available at www.iisd.org/pdf/balatonreport.pdf.

Calgary, City of. 2001. "The FCM Quality of Life Reporting System, Second Report: Quality of Life in Canadian Communities, Calgary Summary." Policy and Planning Division, City of Calgary, Alberta. Also available at www.calgary.ca/DocGallery/BU/community/fcm_quality_life.pdf.

_____. 2000. *Indices of Community Well-Being for Calgary Community Districts*. Calgary, Alberta: Policy and Planning Division. Also available at content.calgary.ca/CCA/City+Hall/Business+Units/Community+Strategies/Publications/Indices+of+Community+Well-Being/Indices+of+Community+Well-Being.htm.

Center for Building Better Communities. 2001. *Hernando County Economic Development Plan*. Gainesville, Florida: University of Florida, Urban and Regional Planning Department.

City of Santa Monica. 2003. *Santa Monica Sustainable City Plan*. Available at www.santa-monica.org/environment/policy/SCP2003.pdf.

Clark, David, Brian Ilbery, and Nigel Berkerley. 1995. "Telematics and Rural Business: An Evaluation of Uses, Potentials and Policy Implications." *Regional Studies* 29: 171–180.

Cobb, Clifford. 2000. *Measurement Tools and the Quality of Life*. San Francisco: Redefining Progress.

_____. 2002. Acting Director, Common Assets Program, Redefining Progress, Sacramento, Calif. Telephone interview with author, October 2.

Cobb, Clifford, and Craig Rixford. 1998. *Lessons Learned From the History of Social Indicators*. San Francisco: Redefining Progress. Also available at www.rprogress.org/publications/pdf/SocIndHist.pdf.

Commonwealth Energy. 1999. "City Of Santa Monica And Commonwealth Energy Sign Deal For Green Power." Press release, May 19. Also available at www.eere.energy.gov/greenpower/santa_399_pr.html.

Cook, Derek. 2002. Policy Planner, Policy and Planning Division, City of Calgary, Alberta. Personal interview with author, July 2.

Couture, Gerry. 2002. Planner, City of Winnipeg, Manitoba. Telephone interview with author, October 16.

Crooks, James B. 2000. "Twenty-Five Years Together: JCCI and the City." [Accessed August 21, 2003]. Available at www.jcci.org/history.htm.

Diener, Ed, and Eunkook Suh. 1997. "Measuring Quality of Life: Economic, Social and Subjective Indicators." *Social Indicators Research* 40, no. 1–2: 189–216.

Douglas, Mary. 1982. *Essays in the Sociology of Perception*. London: Routledge and Kegan Paul.

Federation of Canadian Municipalities (FCM). 2003. Homepage for FCM. [Accessed August 25]. Available at www.fcm.ca/.

Garoogian, Rhoda, Andrew Garoogian, and Patrice Walsh Weingart. 1998. *America's Top-Rated Cities: A Statistical Handbook*. Boca Raton, Fla.: Universal Reference Publications.

Gelb, Richard. 2002. Director, Office of Sustainability and Environment, City of Seattle, Washington. Telephone interview with author, October 10.

Global Reporting Initiative. 2002. *2002 Sustainability Reporting Guidelines*. [Accessed August 26, 2003]. Available at www.globalreporting.org/guidelines/2002.asp.

Greater Vancouver Regional District. 2001. *2001 Annual Report, Livable Region Strategic Plan*. Burnaby, B.C.: Policy and Planning Department, GVRD.

Haines, Anna, and Gary Paul Green. 2002. *Asset Building and Community Development*. Thousand Oaks, Calif.: Sage Publications.

Hardi, Peter, and Laszlo Pinter. 1995. *Models and Methods of Measuring Sustainable Development Performance*. Winnipeg, Manitoba: International Institute of Sustainable Development.

Hardi, Peter and Stephan Barg with Tony Hodge and Laszlo Pinter. 1997. *Measuring Sustainable Development: Review of Current Practice*. Ottawa, Ontario: Industry Canada. Also available at strategis.ic.gc.ca/pics/ra/op17-a.pdf.

Hardi, Peter, and Terrence Zdan, eds. 1997. *Assessing Sustainable Development: Principles in Practice*. Winnipeg, Manitoba: International Institute for Sustainable Development. Also available at iisd1.iisd.ca/pdf/bellagio.pdf.

Hart, Maureen. 2003. "What Is an Indicator of Sustainability?" [Accessed August 26]. Available at www.sustainablemeasures.com/Indicators/WhatIs.html.

Heinz Center for Science, Economics, and the Environment. 2002. *The State of the Nation's Ecosystems: Measuring the Lands, Waters, and Living Resources of the United States*. Cambridge: Cambridge University Press. Also available at www.heinzctr.org/ecosystems/report.html.

Hollander, Justin. 2002. "Measuring Community: Using Sustainability Indicators in Devens, Massachusetts." *Planners' Casebook* 39, Winter: 1–7.

Innes, Judith E. 1998. "Information in Communicative Planning." *Journal of the American Planning Association* 64, no. 1: 52–63.

Innes, Judith E., and Booher, D. E. 2000. "Indicators for Sustainable Communities: A Strategy for Building on Complexity Theory and Distributed Intelligence." *Planning Theory and Practice* 1, no. 2: 173–186.

International Center for Integrative Studies (ICIS). 1999. "Integrated Assessment Models: Uncertainty, Quality and Use." Working Paper I99-E005, ICIS and Maastricht University. March.

International Center for Sustainable Cities (ICSC). 2001. "In Search of Complete Communities: The Journey to Sustainability." Discussion paper presented to the Greater Vancouver Regional District Social Workshop. March.

International Council for Local Environmental Initiatives (ICLEI). 2000. *Measuring Progress: Cities21 Pilot Project Final Report*. Toronto, Ontario: ICLEI.

International Institute for Sustainable Development. 2003. "Compendium: A Global Directory to Indicator Initiatives." [Accessed August 19]. Available at www.iisd.org/measure/compendium.

Keough, Noel. 2002. Director, Sustainable Calgary, Calgary, Alberta. Personal interview with author, July 2.

Kingsley, Thomas. 2002. Researcher, Urban Institute, Washington, D.C. Telephone interview with author October 2.

_____. 1998. "Neighborhood Indicators: Taking Advantage of the New Potential." Paper presented to the American Planning Association National Planning Conference, Boston. April.

Kingsley, Thomas, Claudia Coulton, Michael Barndt, David Sawicki, and Peter Tatian. 1997. *Mapping Your Community: Using Geographic Information to Strengthen Community Initiatives*. Washington, D.C.: U.S. Department of Housing and Urban Development.

Kubani, Dean. 2002. Director, Environmental Programs Division, Santa Monica, California. Telephone interview with author, October 22.

_____. 2003. Director, Environmental Programs Division, Santa Monica, California. Telephone interview with author, June 12.

Lewis Mumford Center for Comparative Urban and Regional Research, University of Albany. 2003. Map New York project homepage. [Accessed August 12]. Available at www.albany.edu/mumford/mapny/.

Maine Economic Growth Council. 2003. *Measures of Growth 2003: Performance Measures and Benchmarks To Achieve a Vibrant and Sustainable Economy for Maine*. [Accessed August 20]. Available at www.mdf.org/megc/measures/megc2003.pdf.

Maser, Elise. 2002. Former Project Manager, Truckee Meadows Regional Planning District, Reno, Nevada. Telephone interview with author, October 15.

Meadows, Donella. 1998. *Indicators and Information Systems for Sustainable Development*. Hartland Four Corners, Vt.: Sustainability Institute.

Meyerson, Martin. 1956. "Building the Middle-Range Bridge for Comprehensive Planning." *Journal of the American Institute of Planners* 22, no. 2: 58–64.

Minnesota, State of, Department of Administration. 2003. "Minnesota Milestones: Measures that Matter." [Accessed August 20]. Available at www.mnplan.state.mn.us/mm/index.html.

Money Magazine. 2003. "Best Places to Live."[Accessed August 26]. Available at money.cnn.com/best/bplive/.

Murphy, David A. 1999. "Presenting Community-Level Data in an 'Outcomes and Indicators' Framework: Lessons from Vermont's Experience." *Public Administration Review* 59, no. 1: 76–77.

Murtagh, B. 1998. "Evaluating the Community Impacts of Urban Policy." *Planning Practice and Research* 13, no. 2: 129–138.

Nelson, Allison. 2003. Community Development Manager, Healthy Families Partnership, City of Hampton, Virginia. Telephone interview with author, 23 September.

New York, City of, Department of City Planning. 2002. *2000/2001 Report on Social Indicators*. [Accessed August 20]. Available at www.nyc.gov/html/dcp/html/pub/socind00.html.

O'Connor, Pam. 1999. Speech to the Mayors' Asia-Pacific Environmental Summit, Honolulu, Hawaii. January 31. Also available at www.csis.org/e4e/mayor12oconnor.html.

Oleari, K. 2000. "Making Your Job Easier: Using Whole-System Approaches to Involve the Community in Sustainable Planning and Development." *Public Management* 82, no. 12: 12–16.

O'Looney, John. 2000. *Beyond Maps: GIS and Decision Making in Local Government*. Redlands, Calif.: Environmental Systems Research Institute.

Oregon Progress Board. 1992. *Oregon Benchmarks: Standards for Measuring Statewide Progress and Government Performance.* Salem, Oreg.: Oregon Progress Board.

Oregon Progress Board. 2003. *Is Oregon Making Progress? The 2003 Benchmark Performance Report.* Salem, Oreg.: Oregon Progress Board. Also available at www.econ.state.or.us/opb/2003report/2003bpr.htm.

Phillips, Rhonda. 2002. *Concept Marketing for Communities: Capitalizing on Underutilized Resources to Generate Growth and Development.* Westport, Conn.: Praeger Publishers.

Redefining Progress, Tyler Norris Associates, and Sustainable Seattle. 1997. *The Community Indicators Handbook.* San Francisco: Redefining Progress.

Rijkens-Klomp, Nicole, Marjolein van Asselt, and Jan Rotmans. 2000. "Towards an Integrated Planning Tool for Sustainable Cities." International Centre for Integrative Studies, Maastricht, Netherlands. Also available at www.icis.unimaas.nl/publ/downs/00_67.pdf.

Rosenfeld, Stuart. 1992. "Key Challenges Facing Rural America." In U.S. General Accounting Office, *Rural Development: Rural America Faces Many Challenges*, GAO/RCED-93-35. Gaithersburg, Md.: GAO, pp. 63–69.

Santa Monica, City of, Environmental Programs Division. 1997. "Santa Monica Sustainable City Program: Sustainability Indicators." [Accessed August 25, 2003]. Available at www.santa-monica.org/environment/policy/indicators.htm.

Santa Monica, City of. 2003. *Santa Monica Sustainable City Plan.* Update adopted February 11. Also available at www.santa-monica.org/environment/policy/SCP2003.pdf.

Sawicki, David S., and Patrice Flynn. 1996. "Neighborhood Indicators: A Review of the Literature and an Assessment of Conceptual and Methodological Issues." *Journal of the American Planning Association* 62, no. 2: 165–183.

Seasons, Mark. 2001. "Indicators and Regional Planning: Theory and Practice." Paper presented to the Association of Collegiate Schools of Planning Annual Conference, Cleveland, Ohio. November 8.

Seattle, City of. Office of Sustainability and Environment (OSE). 2001. *Sustainable Seattle: Our Defining Challenge.* Seattle, Wash.: City of Seattle.

Seymoar, Nola-Kate, Karen Peachey, and Chris Midgley. 2001. *Sustainable Communities in the Greater Vancouver Regional District.* Vancouver, B.C.: International Centre for Sustainable Cities.

Stein, Jay M. 2000. "Doing Right and Making Money: Attracting Corporate Investment via Social Development—Creating Healthy Communities." *Economic Development Review* 17, no. 1: 36-40.

Sustainable Communities Initiative (SCI). 2003. "A Brief History of the City of Austin Sustainable Communities Initiative." [Accessed August 27]. Available at www.ci.austin.tx.us/sustainable/history.htm.

Swanson, Darren. 2002. Researcher, International Institute for Sustainable Development. Winnipeg, Manitoba. Telephone interview with author, October 8.

U.S. Interagency Working Group on Sustainable Development Indicators. 2001. "Sustainable Development in the United States: An Experimental Set of Indicators." U.S. IWGSDI, Washington, D.C.. September.

Van Asselt, Marjolein B.A., Jan Rotmans, Sandra C.H. Greeuw, and Dale S. Rothman. 2001. "Visions: The Visions Methodology." International Centre for Integrative Studies, Maastricht, Netherlands. April. Also available at www.icis.unimaas.nl/publ/downs/01_07.pdf.

Wackernagel, Mathis, and William Rees. 1996. *Our Ecological Footprint: Reducing Human Impact on the Earth.* Gabriola Island, B.C.: New Society Publishers.

Waddell, Steve. 1995. "Lessons from the Healthy Cities Movement for Social Indicator Development." *Social Indicators Research* 34: 213–235.

WilsonMiller. 2002. *Central Western Communities Sector Plan: Stage 2 Final Report.* Tampa, Fla.: WilsonMiller.

MAKING GREAT COMMUNITIES HAPPEN

The American Planning Association provides leadership in the development of vital communities by advocating excellence in community planning, promoting education and citizen empowerment, and providing the tools and support necessary to effect positive change.

465. Adequate Public Facilities Ordinances and Transportation Management. S. Mark White. August 1996. 80pp.

466. Planning for Hillside Development. Robert B. Olshansky. November 1996. 50pp.

467. A Planners Guide to Sustainable Development. Kevin J. Krizek and Joe Power. December 1996. 66pp.

468. Creating Transit-Supportive Land-Use Regulations. Marya Morris, ed. December 1996. 76pp.

469. Gambling, Economic Development, and Historic Preservation. Christopher Chadbourne, Philip Walker, and Mark Wolfe. March 1997. 56pp.

470/471. Habitat Protection Planning: Where the Wild Things Are. Christopher J. Duerksen, Donald L. Elliott, N. Thompson Hobbs, Erin Johnson, and James R. Miller. May 1997. 82pp.

472. Converting Storefronts to Housing: An Illustrated Guide. July 1997. 88pp.

473. Subdivision Design in Flood Hazard Areas. Marya Morris. September 1997. 62pp.

474/475. Online Resources for Planners. Sanjay Jeer. November 1997. 126pp.

476. Nonpoint Source Pollution: A Handbook for Local Governments. Sanjay Jeer, Megan Lewis, Stuart Meck, Jon Witten, and Michelle Zimet. December 1997. 127pp.

477. Transportation Demand Management. Erik Ferguson. March 1998. 68pp.

478. Manufactured Housing: Regulation, Design Innovations, and Development Options. Welford Sanders. July 1998. 120pp.

479. The Principles of Smart Development. September 1998. 113pp.

480/481. Modernizing State Planning Statutes: The Growing Smart℠ Working Papers. Volume 2. September 1998. 269pp.

482. Planning and Zoning for Concentrated Animal Feeding Operations. Jim Schwab. December 1998. 44pp.

483/484. Planning for Post-Disaster Recovery and Reconstruction. Jim Schwab, et al. December 1998. 346pp.

485. Traffic Sheds, Rural Highway Capacity, and Growth Management. Lane Kendig with Stephen Tocknell. March 1999. 24pp.

486. Youth Participation in Community Planning. Ramona Mullahey, Yve Susskind, and Barry Checkoway. June 1999. 70pp.

489/490. Aesthetics, Community Character, and the Law. Christopher J. Duerksen and R. Matthew Goebel. December 1999. 154pp.

493. Transportation Impact Fees and Excise Taxes: A Survey of 16 Jurisdictions. Connie Cooper. July 2000. 62pp.

494. Incentive Zoning: Meeting Urban Design and Affordable Housing Objectives. Marya Morris. September 2000. 64pp.

495/496. Everything You Always Wanted To Know About Regulating Sex Businesses. Eric Damian Kelly and Connie Cooper. December 2000. 168pp.

497/498. Parks, Recreation, and Open Spaces: An Agenda for the 21st Century. Alexander Garvin. December 2000. 72pp.

499. Regulating Home-Based Businesses in the Twenty-First Century. Charles Wunder. December 2000. 37pp.

500/501. Lights, Camera, Community Video. Cabot Orton, Keith Spiegel, and Eddie Gale. April 2001. 76pp.

502. Parks and Economic Development. John L. Crompton. November 2001. 74pp.

503/504. Saving Face: How Corporate Franchise Design Can Respect Community Identity (revised edition). Ronald Lee Fleming. February 2002. 118pp.

505. Telecom Hotels: A Planners Guide. Jennifer Evans-Crowley. March 2002. 31pp.

506/507. Old Cities/Green Cities: Communities Transform Unmanaged Land. J. Blaine Bonham, Jr., Gerri Spilka, and Darl Rastorfer. March 2002. 123pp.

508. Performance Guarantees for Government Permit Granting Authorities. Wayne Feiden and Raymond Burby. July 2002. 80pp.

509. Street Vending: A Survey of Ideas and Lessons for Planners. Jennifer Ball. August 2002. 44pp.

510/511. Parking Standards. Edited by Michael Davidson and Fay Dolnick. November 2002. 181pp.

512. Smart Growth Audits. Jerry Weitz and Leora Susan Waldner. November 2002. 56pp.

513/514. Regional Approaches to Affordable Housing. Stuart Meck, Rebecca Retzlaff, and James Schwab. February 2003. 271pp.

515. Planning for Street Connectivity: Getting from Here to There. Susan Hardy, Robert G. Paterson, and Kent Butler. May 2003. 95pp.

516. Jobs-Housing Balance. Jerry Weitz. November 2003. 41pp.

517. Community Indicators. Rhonda Phillips. December 2003. 46pp.